LIVING FOR A PURPOSE

B. Toliver Walker

All biblical references are from the King James Version of the Bible unless otherwise noted. Any emphasis within a quotation placed in brackets is the author's addition.

Hope of Vision Publishing
Bridgeport, CT 06605
http://www.hovpub.com

Printed in the United States of America
First Edition

ISBN: 978-1-942871-75-0

TO THE GENERATIONS

I was once young and now am old.
In all my days, I have never known the Lord to
forsake the righteous or leave their
seed destitute and deprived of daily bread.

Inspired and Paraphrased From
Psalm 37:25, KJV

ENDORSEMENTS

Living For A Purpose: The Journey is an amazing and compelling read that will help you truly reflect on the guiding Person, purpose, and principles of one's life. Thank you, Bettye, for letting us into your meditative tank and growth conclusions. It's been helpful and refreshing.

Rev. Dr. Keith A. Savage
Senior Pastor, First Baptist Church Manassas

Living For A Purpose: The Journey is truly a strategic, practical, and spiritual read. Bettye takes you on her journey as someone "called" by the Lord to write and write she did. You will learn so much about your practical life while gaining a deeper knowledge of the Kingdom of God. I say, "bravo" to Bettye the writer and "congratulations" to Bettye the woman of God. This is a quick read but most of all a writing of impact!

Dr. Cheryl A. Hill
Founder, G-Level Christians in the Marketplace

Captivated by this little jam-packed jewel called *"Living for a Purpose: The Journey,"* Bettye has captured the journey we all take as Believers with such accuracy. As Believers we all 'struggle' in uncovering or defining our purpose. No need to search or struggle anymore. To those who find themselves in the 3-stage position of maturity, you will find 'the steps' to your purpose laced on the pages of this book. Beautifully and succinctly staged for all who can read to gain clarity and understanding on how, where, and when it will begin for your preordained purpose. Bettye, thank you, for traversing your obedience and penmanship! To God be the glory!

Dr. Georgette Prime-Godwin, CPLC
CEO, Founder of Godwin International Group

Table of Contents

INTRODUCTION

People write for different reasons. Some write for notoriety, some in pursuit of fortune and fame, and some out of pure passion. I write to give birth to my story and seed, to fulfill my purpose in the earth, and to encourage others through the gift of writing. If I were to summarize the contents of this book, I would first tell you what it is not: It is not a book of fiction, mystery, intrigue or suspense. It is not me trying to tell a salacious story to peak your interests or to pen a best-selling book.

Living For A Purpose: The Journey is a book written from my vantage point. It is an open and honest conversation about life, and all the wonderful and painful lessons learned in between. This particular book is the first in a series of books based on the theme, *Living For A Purpose.* I am especially proud of *The Journey* because I get to share my incredible story as a writer, and how the Lord used this extraordinary gift to reveal my true identity in Him.

For me, identity is especially important because it defined and solidified the things I believe in, what I stand for, and who I am in Christ. Even more so, it lends credibility to my witness, as I seek to impact the lives of those who are not familiar with Jesus Christ. People often say it is the journey, not the destination that counts and I totally agree. I agree, because an important part of my journey was in learning how to walk with God and submit to the idea that Jesus masterfully created and designed my life for a purpose.

The takeaway I hope every reader will glean from my experience is the realization that the only thing that matters in life is who you are in Christ, and who Christ is in you. To that end, I invite you to go on this journey with me. If you find you are anything like I once was—chasing after pipe dreams, trying to figure out life, pursuing all the wrong things for all the wrong reasons—then hopefully this book will inspire you. Undoubtedly, many of you will relate to the stories and experiences I share. However, my stories and experiences are not the basis for this writing. The Lord inspired this writing to speak to generations of believers and non-believers alike.

To the *non-believer,* He wants to be a living witness and testimony of truth in your life. To the *believer,* He wants to be the sole authority of truth and power working in and through your life. It is my prayer that this purposeful writing will accomplish all that the Lord desires, resulting in nothing less than the fruitfulness of your life!

B. Toliver Walker

A Minister of God's Grace

CHAPTER ONE

THE JOURNEY

When I was first learning how to drive, my dad would constantly remind me to pay attention to the signs on the road. *"Follow the signs,"* he would say, *"and they will take you anywhere you need to go."* It was the best piece of practical advice anyone could ever give me, and one I would later cherish fondly as the Lord began to teach me how to follow the signs of divine providence and destiny.

* * *

Every journey in life is different. Mine did not begin at birth as one might suspect. It began the moment I walked down a church aisle to accept Jesus Christ, as my Lord and Savior, at the age of 16. At the time, I did not give much thought to how important a decision that was, how it would impact my life, or how it would help me maneuver the difficult challenges headed my way.

For the most part, I was no different than any other 16-year-old. Young, naive, and impetuous, it never occurred to me how precious life was or how meaningless and empty mine would be without Christ in it. I thought I knew everything and there was nothing any adult could tell me that I did not already know or had not experienced for myself. Of course, the true test of how little I did know occurred the moment I left home to attend Norfolk State College, in the Fall of 1972.

I remember being extremely excited about attending a HBCU (Historically Black College and University), with the hope of broadening my exposure to the Black experience. You see, from the time I was a baby, I had grown up traveling across the country and overseas with military parents at the height of Jim Crow laws and segregation. Instead of talking to me about the realities of racism, my parents chose not to discuss it at all. This approach had both its advantages and disadvantages.

The upside to my parents not talking about the disparities of racism is it shielded me from being traumatized and stigmatized by it. The downside is it planted a false reality of life in my mind. I had grown accustomed to interacting with children from all types of cultures, ethnicities, and stations in life. Not once did I view myself in terms of color or consider my ethnicity an impediment or barrier of difference. In my socialization with other children, I quickly learned that not all of them accepted me. Their parents had taught them to judge me based on the color of my skin.

After my dad's retirement and final tour of duty in Italy in 1962, our family moved back to the States where racism and racial prejudice were in full effect. I remember being stunned by it, completely paralyzed by all the disparities attributed to Black people based on the color of their skin. It was an ideology I was not familiar with or fully prepared for, as my mother enrolled me into a four-room schoolhouse for Black children, called the *Newtown School.*

The Newtown School was one of 5,000 Rosenwald schools built in the segregated South for Black children, funded through "the collaborative efforts of Booker T. Washington and Julius Rosenwald," President of Sears, Roebuck & Company. (McClure, 2018). At the age of 9, I was too shy and introverted to vocalize my feelings and concerns. But what I do know is from that day forward, I was never the same mentally, socially, or psychologically.

The Newtown School lacked many of the educational opportunities I had grown accustomed to from attending military funded and supported schools. Having spent the first nine years of my life participating in some of the best schools and academic curriculum's afforded to military children, I was too far advanced from my peers at the Newtown School. Out of fairness and equity to the other children, my one Black teacher thought it best to keep me on par with the other students. Tragically, over the next two years, I learned nothing new and was not mentally challenged or encouraged to learn anything beyond what I already knew.

By the time the schools integrated in 1965, I had become a slow learner, unable to comprehend or compute the simplest of tasks. For the next six years, I struggled mentally trying to regain some semblance of my former self prior to the Newtown School. After graduating from a predominately white high school, where Blacks represented less than 10% of the school population, I felt thoroughly deprived and stripped of any cultural identity, history, intellect, or relevance. Enrolling into a HBCU offered me an opportunity to rediscover myself and regain a sense of belonging.

Unfortunately, in the course of trying to rediscover my cultural identity, I had completely forgotten about my spiritual identity. My cultural identity only told half the story. There was another side, a spiritual side, that I had yet to discover. I never questioned my faith and belief in God, or my earnest confession of Christ but, the fact remained, I had yet to discover who I was in Christ or who Christ was in me. This was something I had never given any serious thought to because I thought "being saved" was enough.

At best, my relationship with Christ boiled down to a religious experience. An experience where He knew me, but I did not know Him. Since no one had ever bothered to explain the difference between a "religious experience" and an "intimate relationship" with Christ, I did what any well-intentioned college-bound student would do: I slowly drifted away from God, as I settled into college life.

After Norfolk State, I went on to pursue my master's degree in Communications Design at Pratt Institute. The first in my family to go to college, I had high hopes of achieving many of the goals my parents could only dream of. Those dreams were short-lived as I faced the failing health and eventual death of my mother from cancer, my first year.

The manner in which I received the news of her failing health was traumatizing. In the preceding days and weeks leading up to her funeral, I desperately wanted to grieve but was not allowed to. My dad was so traumatized by the loss himself that he became increasingly lethargic and incapable of making any decisions. This left the bulk of planning my mother's funeral squarely in my hands. This was something I never imagined having to do let alone being held responsible for. My mother was my best friend and confidant. She validated me in ways that no one ever could or has since. Now that she was gone, I felt this unbearable emptiness, sadness, and loneliness welling up inside me. With everyone pulling on me to make decisions, I did not have the luxury of falling apart. So, I neatly tucked my feelings of sadness and remorse inside me to do what my dad was incapable of doing.

After the funeral, I was tasked with settling my mother's financial affairs. When my dad realized I was not willing to forego the obligation of paying off her debts to give him the bulk of the money, it created a five-year breach between us—a breach that lasted until a few days prior to his death. The ease at which my dad chose to sever ties with me, coupled with the internalized grief and loss of my mother, wounded me in ways I could not describe.

For the first time in my life, I felt alone and on my own without anyone to guide me. That was the moment I knew I was a novice at life and did not know half as much as I thought I did. If there was any hope of surviving life, then someone greater than me would need to order my steps.

Divine Providence

In the days to follow, it was nothing but divine providence that kept me sane. In my darkest moments, the Lord was always there. No matter how far or often I strayed from Him, He always left a trail of breadcrumbs to guide my way back to Him. I am immensely grateful that nothing—not death, life, principalities, powers, things present, or things to come[1]—could sabotage or change the trajectory of my life. The only reason none of these things had the power to alter my life is because it was *"hid with Christ in God"* (Col. 3:3), the moment I accepted Him at the age of 16.

Having now walked with the Lord for the better part of six decades, I have a deep and profound reverence for divine providence. *Divine providence*, as I understand it now is God's "conceived power to sustain and guide human destiny." (Merriam-Webster.com (a), 2019). Jesus, being equal with God in identity, purpose, and power, holds the distinct honor of being our Creator. The evidence of this is stated in John 1:3 (NKJV): *"All things were made by Him and without Him nothing was made that was made."*

The fact that Jesus is equal with the Father in all things tells me He is equally *omniscient* (all-wise, all-knowing, all-seeing), *omnipotent* (all-powerful, fully capable of achieving anything) and *omnipresent* (present in all places at all times). If Jesus is capable of all these things, then how much more is He capable of keeping me, guiding me, and overseeing the affairs of my life?

A Writer's Journey

The best way I know to explain how divine providence operates throughout the human story is to share my incredible journey as a writer. My journey as a writer began in February 2002. I remember the occasion well because it was marked by an unusual request from the Lord:

"I want you to write a book," He said, **"and call it, Living For A Purpose."**

Those were the last words I heard from Him for the next two years, words that both elated and intimated me. On one hand, I was elated He had chosen me for such a lofty assignment. On the other hand, I was intimated by it because I was not a skilled or trained writer. Asking me to do something I had never done before was forcing me outside my comfort zone. Entertaining His request, without having the first clue of how to get started, sounded so ridiculous I briefly entertained the thought of ignoring Him, pretending as if I had never heard Him.

The only problem was I did hear Him, and there was no getting around that fact. The challenge for me was not so much a matter of knowing *how* to write but *what* to write in trying to explain what *living for a purpose* meant to me. I was 48 years old and had been walking with the Lord for the better part of 32 years. I was saved, Spirit-filled, fully licensed and ordained for ministry. And yet, I had no clue of what it meant to "live for a purpose." It was a completely foreign concept to me and one that I could not articulate. If I could not articulate it, then how could I write about it? If I could not write about it, then what did that say about me as a woman of faith supposedly walking with God?

I had never asked or prayed to be a writer and yet the Lord had chosen me. No matter how unworthy or under qualified I felt about myself or my potential, this was my defining moment. Either I would step up to the plate and rise to the challenge, or cowardly shrink back into some dark corner and give in to defeat. I had a choice to make and there was no getting around the fact that I was the vessel the Lord had chosen to speak to and write through.

Unquestionable Obedience

Consumed with fear, I pleaded with the Lord to provide guidance and instruction on how to write this book, but my pleas appeared to fall on deaf ears. I remember thinking, *"Maybe the Lord is waiting on me to do something."* Out of sheer ignorance, I came up with the ingenious idea to solicit the help of a co-worker (someone I felt was more anointed and spiritually gifted than I was) to co-author the book with me. Since the Lord appeared to pose no objections, I assumed I had His approval. The next thing I know, a major misunderstanding took place between me and my co-worker that caused an irreparable breach in our relationship. A breach so devastating that she not only completely severed ties with me but one that, to this day, I do not know what the cause of it was.

After such a traumatic experience, one would think I would have learned my lesson. Unfortunately, wisdom was not my strongest attribute back then. Not long after the devastating break with my co-worker I was back at it again, relying on my human instincts and intelligence to accomplish what the Lord was asking. This time, I decided to enroll in a writing class to acquire the necessary training and skills I needed to write the book. Oddly enough, I never found the time or money to enroll into the course. With no other options available, I finally got down on my knees and began to cry out to the Lord:

"Ok, Lord. I know I heard Your voice. Thing is, I do not know how to accomplish what You ask. Everything I have tried has failed. So, if You want me to write this book, then You are going to have to teach me how to write," I prayed.

Not long after that prayer, the Lord began to speak to me, sometimes sharing only a few words at a time. At other times, uttering complete phrases, thoughts, and ideas; or engaging me in full conversations. This is the moment, I recognized this was no ordinary writing assignment. All this time, the Lord had been grooming me to write in partnership with Him, so He could express His thoughts and heart through my experiences. From that day until now, I write in partnership with Him, listening ever so closely for His small still voice speaking through the Holy Spirit.

Pulling Down Strongholds

Several months later, I was no farther along in my writing than the day I first heard the Lord's voice. A thousand questions were swirling around in my head. Where do I begin? How do I explain a life that was not of my choosing? A life that has left me childless, unmarried, nearly fifty years old, and yet called and chosen of God? Do I write from a position of weakness and reveal the truth behind my fears? Or do I write from a position of strength and share the wisdom of my years?

Outwardly, I was a model Christian: Stoic, poised, and on fire for God. Inwardly, I was a broken shattered mess, haunted by a past I did not want to confront but could not let go of. All the hardships, sadness, and trauma I had endured had finally caught up with me. It was the fake facade I wore every day—a facade that kept me handicapped and in bondage for a good portion of my life.

Instead of confronting my past, I neatly tucked it away inside me trying to survive it. The same way I had tried to survive the death of my mother and my abandonment by my dad. Meanwhile, the Lord was working in the background, speaking through my writing, peeling back all the layers, and trying to teach me how to unapologetically talk about the parts of my life I considered personal and private.

It was a day of reckoning for me. The day when I stopped running from my past and began to face it. The Lord wanted me to be free. He knew the only way I could be free was to find a sense of wholeness in Him. The first step towards my freedom was to stop glamorizing my strongholds, by pretending as if they did not exist or did not bother me. I had to confront them, confessing each one outright, and replacing each lie with the truth of God's word.

As I slowly relinquished each one, I remembered the words from 2 Corinthians 10:4-6 (NKJV): *"For the weapons of our warfare are not carnal but mighty in God for pulling down strongholds, casting down arguments and every high thing that exalts itself against the knowledge of God, bringing every thought into captivity to the obedience of Christ, and being ready to punish all disobedience when your obedience is fulfilled."*

I repeated the passage, over and over again in my mind, until I could feel my spirit rising, pulling itself up, and steadying itself in an upright position. As I slowly regained my strength, I began to take authority over every stronghold in my life, placing it under the authority and subjection of Christ. It was the start of a new way of thinking and living for me, one founded upon the love of life and not shame.

Divine Intervention

The Lord saw something in me that I did not see in myself. Lying dormant inside me was His seed. His seed reverberated in me that I was a person of great value to Him. A person who had been prohibited from embracing her future because she was held captive by her past. The painful truth is, I had allowed it. I had allowed the spirit of low self-esteem to govern my life. Without realizing it, I had given license to the devil to manipulate and control me, stealing my identity, until I lost sight of who I was.

In many ways, I became a beggar. Someone so poor, despised, and utterly worthless in my own eyes that I thought I had no real value or purpose in life. In my heart, I wanted to do better and be better, but I did not know how. That was the moment the Lord stepped in, taking matters into His own hands, and launching me on a 17-year-journey (2002–

2019) to teach me what living for a purpose was all about. In the course of those 17 years, patience had her "perfect work" in me, until I became "perfect [whole] and complete, lacking nothing." (Jam. 1:4). In the end, the journey proved more valuable than I could ever imagine, for it exposed the magnificent seed of God inside my story.

The Passenger's View

I thought I had it all together spiritually, but the Lord knew otherwise. Deep down inside, I was fearful of the eventualities of life and all the things beyond my control. To show just how far off I was in understanding the nature of our relationship, the Lord staged an intervention. On this particular day, I was resting comfortably in my recliner at home, slightly dozing off when suddenly I saw a vision of myself riding in an open convertible with the Lord.

In the vision, the Lord appeared as an ordinary man and someone I felt extremely comfortable and safe with. He was in the driver's seat steering the car with one hand on the wheel, while I was resting comfortably in the passenger's seat with my eyes closed, and head tilted back on the headrest. It was a beautiful, warm, sunny day. Every so often, I would open my eyes to capture a glimpse of the tree-lined street we were traveling on with quaint little shops on either side. I felt completely pampered in His company but quickly became anxious. Overly concerned that the ride was taking too long and we might be lost, I started offering suggestions on where to go, to take advantage of any shortcuts or alternative routes to hasten our trip.

Needless to say, the Lord never told me where we were going and I never bothered to ask. Still, I felt this overwhelming compulsion to give Him advice, without having any knowledge of what the final destination was. In the sweetest kindest voice, the Lord turned to me and said:

"Bettye, just relax and enjoy the scenery. I've got this. Here, enjoy some of the snacks I bought for you. You are going to love where I am taking you!" He said.

In His own unique and wonderful way, the Lord was providing me with a real-life scenario of our relationship to one another. In real-life, He was taking me on a journey. A journey which spelled out in no uncertain terms that I had not entered into a place of rest with Him. He felt no compulsion to reveal where we were going because He was the Way. His relationship with me was perfect. Unfazed by my lack of faith and trust in Him, He had remained consistently loving, kind, and unwavering in driving me to where I needed to go.

My relationship with Him, on the other hand, was atrocious. Symptomatic of someone immature, unsettled, and anxious, I had subconsciously tried to take the wheel from Him on numerous occasions, trying to direct the course of my own life. The beauty of His relationship with me is He never judged or rebuked me for my poor behavior. Instead, He lovingly took the time to show me the areas in my life that required further adjustment and discipline. As a result of this vision, I learned three important things about myself in relation to the Lord's divine nature:

Believe in Him. The Lord knows me and is always mindful of me. I can believe Him because His nature is nothing like man. He is a *"God of truth"* (Deut. 32:4). He *"cannot lie"* (Tit. 1:2). He is not *"human, so He does not change his mind."* (Num. 23:19, NLT). The Bible says, *"But without faith it impossible to please him: for he that cometh to God must believe that He is, and that He is a rewarder of them that diligently seek Him."* (Heb. 11:6).

Trust Him. Nothing escapes the Lord. Nothing gets past Him. And no one in heaven, on earth, or in hell can deceive Him, for He is: *"Alpha and the Omega—the beginning and the end...the Lord God....who is, who always was, and who is still to come—the Almighty One."* (Rev. 1:8; Cp. Exo. 3:14; 6:2). If the Lord knows who I am and what my needs are, then I can trust in His ability to guide my footsteps, direct my path in life, and cause all things to *"work together for my good."*[2]

Far too often, we place more trust and confidence in human beings than we do in God. When things go wrong as a result of our choices, we immediately want to blame God for it. When in reality, the fault is entirely ours in choosing not to seek the face of God for advice, guidance, and instruction in the first place.

Enter Into His Rest. Being anxious, restless, and unsettled is sheer torment. Coming into a place of rest in Christ means that I am placing all my confidence in His ability to protect, deliver, and carry me in times of trouble, difficulty, and adversity. Instead of fretting over the things I cannot change or questioning the Lord's ability to work on my behalf, the correct approach would be to ask for His guidance that He might grant me the wisdom to maneuver through any challenge I encounter.

The Lord has promised to withhold *"no good thing"* from those *"who walk uprightly"* before Him. (Psa. 84:11). Therefore, I can rest in the *"quiet confidence"* [3] of His strength and not my own.

CHAPTER TWO

THE DISCIPLINES

When I was in my mid-to-late twenties, I struggled with all sorts of uncertainties about life. On one occasion, I was so overwhelmed and frustrated that I decided to schedule an appointment with my then pastor, Apostle Ralph G. Nichol, to gain some clarity and insight into my situation.

On the day of our meeting, I poured my heart out to him, unloading what seemed like a barrage of issues and concerns that weighed heavily on my heart. Listening intently, Apostle Nichol lowered his head as if in private consultation with the Lord. After I finished speaking, he lifted his head, stared at me intently, and offered this single piece of advice:

"Bettye put your hand in God's hand and walk with Him. Don't move ahead of God and don't lag behind Him. Walk side-by-side and hand-in-hand with God. If He moves to the left, then you move to the left. If He moves to the right, then you move to the right. Whichever way God is leading that is the direction you should follow," he said.

I left Apostle Nichol's office that day, disappointed that I had not received the response I was hoping for. Later in life, I would come to appreciate the wonderful gift he had given me by example. In a very unassuming way, Apostle Nichol had taught me two important disciplines in life, that of learning how to seek the Lord's counsel in all matters and learning how to walk with God.

* * *

The manner in which Apostle Nichol prayerfully addressed my concerns left such an impression on me that it marked a significant turning point in my life. From that day forward, I unknowingly became a student of discipline. The kind of discipline that makes a person take stock in how God is moving, working, and operating at all times in life; and one that required both my participation, conformity, and compliance to the will of God and a godly code of conduct. As I sought the Lord for a greater understanding of *discipline* (what it is and how it works) I came into the understanding that it had nothing to do with me being saved, knowing the Bible, or being spiritually discerning.

What Is Discipline?

According to blog site Focus 3, the word *discipline* is derived from the Latin word *disciplina*, meaning "instruction and training." The word, *disciplina* is a derivative of the root word *discere*, which means "to learn." So then, to adhere to discipline "is to study, learn, train, and apply a system of standards" to one's life. [It is not] rules, regulations, or punishment. It is not compliance, obedience, or enforcement. It is not rigid, boring, or always doing the same thing. [It is not] obedience to someone else's standards to avoid punishment...discipline is a choice, "the choice you make in learning and applying intentional standards to achieve meaningful objectives."[4] [It is] not something others do to you. It is something you do for yourself." (Focus 3, LLC, 2019).

Understanding Discipline

Instruction and guidance can come from any number of sources, including various life experiences or forms of instructional training. However, discipline it is not an external experience. It is an internal one. It is a means to an end. A way to transition us from one stage of development to another. It is the acquisition of wisdom, knowledge, and understanding; and our adherence to a code of conduct that results in corrective behavior and transformation.

Generally speaking, a *code of conduct* is thought to be a "set of rules outlining the norms, responsibilities, proper etiquette, and practices." (Wikipedia, 2020). A good model to explain this is the process of sanctification. If *sanctification* (the process of being set apart and made holy for the Lord's use) is the chief goal and objective in life, then *discipline* would be the means through which the Lord would help us to achieve it. In other words, the Lord works through certain experiences in our lives to address our shortcomings. Discipline then becomes an invaluable tool in helping to bring us into compliance with the will of God, God's standards, and God's code of conduct.

It is the thing that drives our direction in life, enables us to make better choices and decisions in life. Moreover, it is the principle way the Lord molds us into vessels of *"honor, sanctified, and fit [properly equipped] for the master's use, and prepared unto every good work."* (2 Tim. 2:21). The process itself can be a long and arduous one, often taking years and sometimes a lifetime to manifest. Truth be told, there is no instant gratification derived from discipline.

Submitting to it, forces us outside our comfort zone to act responsibly as adults. Avoiding it, sabotages any effort to refine and define our character, purpose, and identity. And without it, spiritual growth and development is nearly impossible. Despite how any of us may feel about discipline, there are only a few reasons anyone would choose to avoid it: One, they are too arrogant and proud to admit they need it; two, they are unwilling to let go of their egos long enough to submit to the "will of God" (Rom. 12:2); or three, they have deluded themselves into thinking they can address their problems and issues on their own, without any help or assistance from God.

The reality of the latter is our human nature is woefully flawed and fallible. We are incapable of self-diagnosis or employing the right corrective measures to match God's standards and expectation for change. Not to mention, our incompetence when it comes to transforming ourselves into an equivalent of God's nature and character, without His expressed help. To the contrary, the Lord works through our human experiences and discipline, to renew, transform, and fashion our minds after the mind of Christ[5] and the perfect will of God.

The Necessity of Discipline

The key advantage of discipline is it helps sharpen our mental, physical, and spiritual acuity. It unites our triune nature—body, soul, and spirit—bringing it into compliance with the harmony and oneness of God. When the human soul becomes one with God, then the Lord is free to order our steps unencumbered. This is essentially what is implied in Psalm 37:23: *"The steps of a good man are ordered by the LORD: and he delighteth in His way."*

Jesus can influence our steps, but He cannot act against our free-will without our permission, consent, and cooperation. We *delight* in His ways (or please Him), when we surrender our will to the will of the Father. Then, and only then, is Jesus free to order our steps for our good. This, in a nutshell, is the primary reason many believers do not know who they are, what their calling is, or what God's express purpose is for their lives; and why the Lord is often prohibited from conveying the will, wisdom, and knowledge of God to them.

Disciplining the body[6] and mind[7] was a common theme throughout Paul's teachings. He considered it of such great importance that he regarded it as a reasonable expectation of anyone in God's service: *"I beseech you brethren, by the mercies of God that ye present your bodies a living sacrifice, holy, acceptable unto God, which is your reasonable service; and be not conformed to this world: but be ye transformed by the renewing of your mind, that ye may prove what is that good, and acceptable, and perfect, will of God."* (Rom. 12:1-2).

Paul did not advocate for discipline to needlessly impose a stringent lifestyle upon other fellow believers. He advocated for it because he believed anyone who regarded themselves as a member of Christ's body was automatically called to exemplify that which is *"good, acceptable, and perfect"* according to the *"will of God."* (v.2).

My Twelve Disciplines

Understanding Paul's pragmatic approach helped me to identify some of the important disciplines that had occurred in my own life. Of course, I did not immediately recognize them as such or as they occurred in my life. I only recognized them after reflecting on the things that influenced my life, reshaped my thinking, and subsequently taught me wisdom. As I began to think back on all the disciplines that had influenced my life, I came across at least twelve that personally benefited me in some way:

(1) *Defining Church*

In the mid-to-late 1980s, the idea of being called and chosen for a divine purpose was practically unheard of. Most spiritual leaders rarely broached the subject of purpose because they either did not understand what it was or simply refused to acknowledge it, for fear of losing control over their congregations. The first time I heard anything about the possibility of being called and chosen for a God-ordained purpose was in the early '90s, through the anointed teachings of Dr. Miles Monroe. Prior to that, I was doing what every Believer in those days did, which was to serve God through my devotion and support of the local church.

I have no regrets for doing so because the local church was my starting place. It was the place where I became an advocate of the gospel, developed a passion for soul-winning, and acquired an interest in prison ministry, evangelistic outreach, counseling, and intercessory prayer. It was the place where I established a foundation in Christ, became an avid student of the Word, developed moral and ethical standards, and learned to walk uprightly as a person of principle before God.

Understanding the difference between the *Church* (the body of Christ) versus the *church* (the local church)—what it is and how it functions—was an important discipline to learn because it helped clarify the difference between faith and religion. Case in point: Over the course of my life, I have been influenced by certain philosophies like Buddhism and Transcendental Meditation, as well as Christian-based churches like Catholicism, United Methodist, Pentecostal, Non-Denominational, and Baptist.

However, none of these experiences proved to be as expedient or impactful as my initial encounter with the presence of God, while attending church services at Deliverance Evangelistic Centers, Inc. in Newark, New

Jersey. I had been invited by one of my neighbors to visit the church since I was currently not attending any church. The moment I entered the sanctuary, I was immediately struck by the prayers being offered up on behalf of the people by the saints of God, who were gathered around the altar.

The nature of their prayers was unlike anything I had ever heard or experienced before. There was a fluidity to it that flowed like incense, permeating the air and flowing up into the nostrils of God. I could literally feel the presence and glory of God in the building. In return for their reverence and worship of God, the Holy Spirit moved in an unusual and miraculous way during the church service.

Still young, impetuous, and in my mid-twenties, I had not stepped foot in a church since I left home for college. Sensing the presence of God for myself made the reality of a triune God (Father, Son, and Holy Spirit), real and tangible. As I took my seat mid-way of the center row of pews, I felt the warmth of His presence envelope me and I knew immediately, this was not a religious experience.

I could not explain it but could not deny it. After such a profound experience, I knew that nothing—no church, denomination, or religious experience—could ever rival or equal the powerful experience of being in the presence of God. I knew instantly, this was that intimate relationship with Christ I had been searching for all my life. The experience so thoroughly satisfied my curiosity of God that I am convinced, no one can ever truly know or comprehend the *"breadth, length, depth, or height"* (Eph. 3:18) of a relationship with God, through Jesus Christ,[8] unless they experienced Him for themselves.

(2) A Human Perspective of Church

Being reminded of such a precious memory made me think more circumspectly about my own perceptions of the local church. For many years, I held the longstanding view that the local church was disjointed, fueled by political influence, personal bias, hypocritical behavior and a great deal of monetizing. I believed the local church had lost its saltiness[9] in producing seasoned candidates for the work of the ministry; and was increasingly becoming ineffective as a vehicle for teaching, training, and launching fully developed disciples.

However, as the Lord began to speak to me concerning the nature of the Church He established, I realized my perspective of the local church was unjustly harsh and skewed in perspective. From a human standpoint, it is easy to cast stones at the local church for all of its misgivings, missteps, and erroneous ways. We can even fall prey to the ideology that the local church is no longer relevant, relatable, or reputable; or that it is supposed to be some perfect infallible institution of faith, designed to meet all our spiritual needs.

The local church was never meant to be (nor can it ever be) a suitable substitute for Jesus Christ. It is merely a catalyst, one of many venues used to promote the gospel and teachings of Christ. At best, it is a gathering place for believers to convene, fellowship, worship, be edified, and establish a foundation in Christ. It is not equipped to satisfy all the spiritual needs of every person, for only Jesus is empowered to do that. If our focus, loyalty, devotion, and dependence is placed on anything or anyone, it should be Jesus. No matter how grand, prestigious, or anointed a person may be, they cannot take the place of Jesus. They are mere vessels through whom the Lord chooses to work, and speak to establish His Kingdom on earth.

No local church, denomination or religion can ingratiate us into the favor of God, for there is only one Mediator between God and man, and that is Jesus Christ.[10] Instead of demonizing the local church for its failings and misgivings, we need to appreciate it for all the many offerings it does bring, in context of what it is designed to do and how it is meant to serve. However imperfect or fallible we may believe the local church to be, it does serve a purpose in our lives. The lesson the Lord wanted to teach me is the local church had accomplished exactly what it was meant to do in my life; which was to serve as a foundation to train and development me spiritually. At minimum, the local church accomplishes three things in our lives:

It Serves Us. As a local hub and gathering place, the local church was established to serve as a safe haven for the unsaved to experience the love of God and the presence of God through the example and fellowship of the saints. It is the place where believers can fellowship, worship, be trained, and edified with other like-minded individuals. It is the place where we can openly confess our sins, fears, anxieties, and shortcomings in an atmosphere of grace. The place where we gather to be healed, delivered and grow exponentially in faith, love and hope. In light of the many things the local church does offer, the Lord expects us to replicate the same in others until there is no need, want, or lack within the body of Christ or the local church.

It Feeds Us. The local church is designed to be a place of healing, hope, nourishment, and deliverance. It is the place where we are to receive all the necessary nutritional supplements to keep us healthy, whole and of sound mind. Within its walls, we derive a deeper understanding of the gospel, discover the fundamentals of life building and spiritual enrichment, and learn how to become a mirror image of Jesus Christ. More importantly, it is a place of exchange. The Bible says, *"present your bodies a living sacrifice, holy, acceptable unto God."* (Rom. 12:1). In exchange for all the *preparatory work* we acquire as a result of the local church's efforts, we should be more than willing to allow the Holy Spirit to refine us and develop us for service in either a five-fold[11] capacity or some other form of ministry support.[12]

It Develops Us. Every mature member of the body of Christ is responsible for three fundamental tasks: To *"perfect the saints"* until they come into full maturity; promote and engage *"the work of the ministry,"* and; morally and spiritually *"edify"* (advise, instruct, embolden) *"the body of Christ"* until they yield fruit. (Eph. 4:12).

(3) A Kingdom Perspective of Church

A Kingdom mindset is best understood through the example of Jesus Christ. Jesus never did anything randomly or unintentionally. Every word He spoke had a purpose. Every miracle He performed was intentional. Every aspect of his personality and character exhibited the nature and principles of the Kingdom. If our objective is to follow Jesus and be His example, then everything we do should be Kingdom minded.

One of the key identifiable attributes of Kingdom-minded individuals is their focus and interests are always towards the Kingdom. All decision-making and efforts are God-centered; and all outward acts of love, hope, and faith are people-centered. Kingdom-minded individuals generally have a keen sense of who they are, what they are called to, and where the Lord desires for them to serve. They are often found serving in capacities where the need is greatest and where their service can be of greatest impact on behalf of the Kingdom.

Other definable characteristics are the specific capacities in which they serve. For example, if called to minister to the unsaved and unbelieving, they are often drawn to service-oriented positions that offer the greatest potential for reaching and influencing those who are lost, destitute, unlearned, uninformed, impoverished, and/or disconnected from God. If called to minister to the saved and believing, they are often drawn to service-oriented positions that offer the greatest potential for reaching and influencing members of the body of Christ, the local church, leaders, entrepreneurs, and/or marketplace engagement.

The difference in approach between a human mindset and a kingdom mindset boils down to a matter of whether a person has been indoctrinated into a local church or engrafted into the body of Christ. Those who are indoctrinated, generally care for the things that serve to promote the agenda of the local church, a denomination, or religious organization. Whereas, those who have been engrafted, generally care more for the needs, longevity, and promotion of the Kingdom.

This is an important distinction to make because Jesus did not come to proclaim and promote His own agenda. He came to establish and promote the Kingdom of God[13] here on earth. This concept can only be understood from God's perspective: The Kingdom of God, which is comprised solely of Kingdom-minded people—that is to say, individuals who represent the body of Christ—is a construct patterned after the nature and characteristics of the Kingdom of Heaven.

The Kingdom of God is autonomous in that it functions as a self-governing entity, operating under the control, auspices, and direction of Jesus Christ, the Head of the entire body. So, simply by virtue of their very nature (who they represent and who they are aligned with), Kingdom-minded individuals have a strong constitution when it comes to faithfulness, fruitfulness, spiritual maturity, and being rooted in the principles and practices of the Kingdom.

They understand the necessity of going *"into all the world"* to *"preach the gospel to every creature"* (Mrk. 16:15) because their confidence does not lie in their own abilities or potential, but in the faithfulness of Jesus to confirm every "word" He speaks through them *"with signs following."* (Mrk. 16:20; Cp. Mat. 24:14).

Notice, Jesus did not tell us to remain hidden behind the comfortable and convenient walls of the local church, our preferred denomination, or favorite congregation. He said, *"Go ye into the world and preach the gospel."* (Mrk. 16:15). The word *all* suggests a worldwide and global infiltration of the "good news" of Jesus Christ.

Going into the *world* requires strategic warfare. A type of warfare that is planned, deliberate, calculated, and targeted over a period of time, until certain goals and interests are accomplished. It involves the forward movement and advancement of the Kingdom to engage a ruthless enemy on his turf, fighting fiercely on behalf of those who are defenseless and cannot fight for themselves.

This level of spiritual fighting is not for the fearful, weak or meek; and neither can we avoid it. To the contrary, it is an *anticipated expectation* and *reality* of every believer. Not only should we anticipate it, we should also come fully prepared and equipped to defend our cause when called upon to do so. We are not helpless, hopeless or powerless in this effort, for the Lord has given us every weapon, tool, and resource we need to fight and win. Listen to what Jesus said about spiritual warfare: *"From the days of John the Baptist until now the kingdom of heaven suffereth violence, and the violent take it by force."* (Mat. 11:12).

He also said, *"It is not for you to know the times or the seasons, which the Father hath put in his own power. But ye shall receive power, after that the Holy Ghost is come upon you: and ye shall be witnesses unto me both in Jerusalem, and in all Judaea, and in Samaria, and unto the uttermost part of the earth."* (Act 1:7-8).

We are aligned with a far superior Church defined by Jesus, Himself. He did not call and choose us to be indoctrinated into some church, denomination, or religion. He called and chose us to represent the Kingdom in an empirical way.[14] If our goal is to become the Church that Jesus built, then two things must happen: One, we must not be so quick to judge others, for there is only One who has the authoritative power to judge what He created and that is Jesus. Jesus openly declared to the Father that He knows who belongs to Him and is a part of His body: *"Of those whom You gave me I have lost none."* (John 18:9, NKJV).

Two, our alignment with the Church that Jesus established automatically subjects us to the laws of the Kingdom. Therefore, we should never allow ourselves to be defined, confined, or restrained by the deficiencies, dealings, or inner workings of some man-made institution or brick and mortar building.

(4) The Nature of Priestly Service

As Kingdom-minded individuals, our first priority is to be a holy habitation and dwelling place for the Holy Spirit. Secondly, we are to "live, move, and have our being" in Christ. Thirdly, and most importantly, we are to be led by His Spirit, to go wherever He sends us and serve wherever and however He has need of us. This is, the nature, essence and expectation of priestly service.[15] It is extremely important then, for us to understand the necessity of transitioning from a "holy place" (as faithful members of a local church), to enter into the "most holy place" (where we dwell and abide in the presence of God forever). The Bible says, *"He that dwelleth in the secret place of the Most High shall abide under the shadow of the Almighty."* (Psa. 91:1). This level of commitment requires a *priestly* form of service.

The Old Testament Tabernacle presents us with a perfect illustration of the spiritual and progressive nature of a priestly servant. "To an age that knew little about God,

Figure 1: The Old Testament Tabernacle

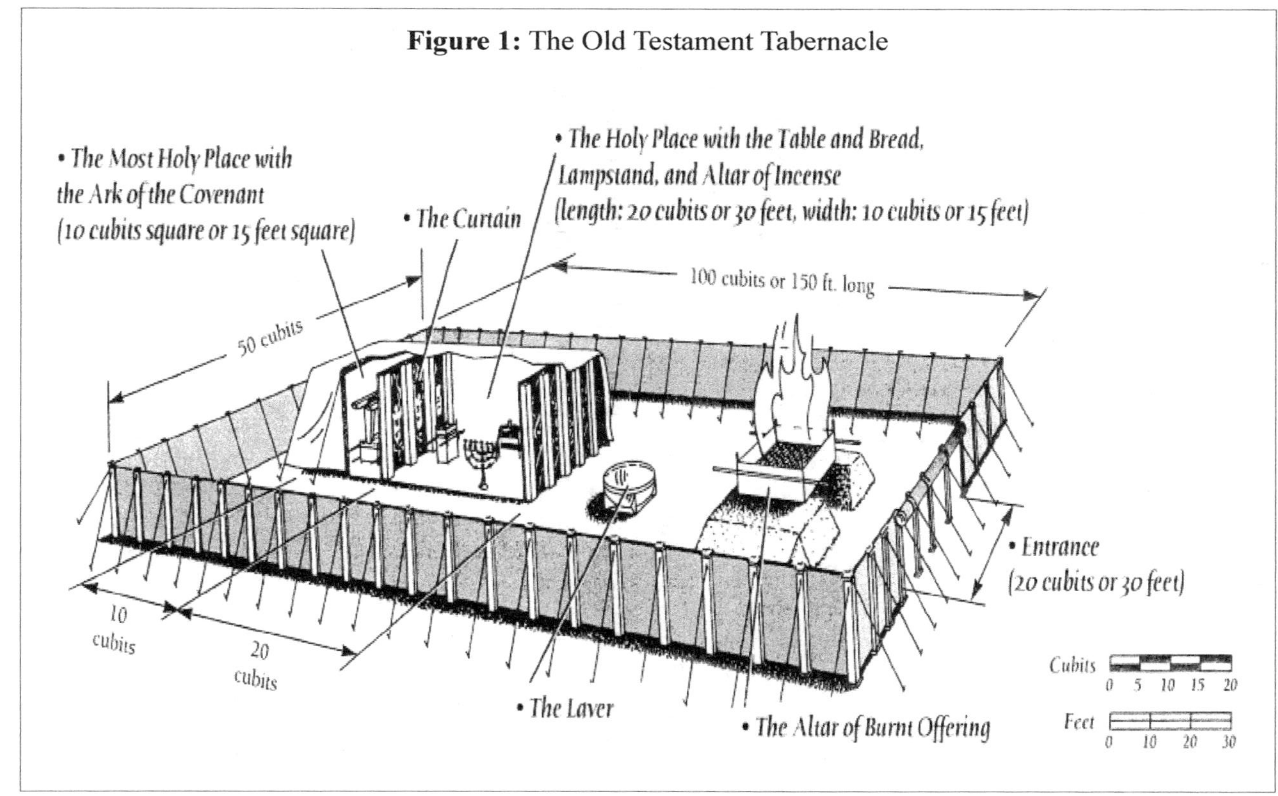

the Tabernacle showed the way to communion with God and foreshadowed the coming of the great high priest, the Lord Jesus Christ. The central truths surrounding God's redemptive process have never changed." (NetBibleStudy.com, n.d.). Salvation can only be accessed through one entrance, gate and door which is Jesus Christ. All who choose to follow Him must be willing to surrender to a life of sacrifice and sanctification in the *outer court.* They must have a posture of prayer, worship, and service in the *holy place.* The level of intimacy required in the *most holy place* can only be achieved through a one-to-one relationship with God, through Jesus Christ—a level of intimacy where we no longer look to humanity for support and guidance, but rather look to Jesus, *"the founder and perfecter of our faith."* (Heb. 12:2, ESV).

The same can be said of the spiritual makeup of priestly servants. They mirror the image of Christ in both word, deed, and example; they are fully functional members of the body of Christ, *"speaking the truth in love,"* so others *"may grow up into Him in all things"* (Eph. 4:15); and they are vessels of honor[16] that God can use to replicate the Kingdom on earth, according to the nature and pattern of Heaven.[17] Equally so, is the nature of their character which is progressive, revolutionary, and evolutionary: They are *progressive* in the sense that they are willing to *"present their bodies as a living sacrifice, holy, [and] acceptable unto God"* (Rom. 12:1). They are *revolutionary* in the sense that they enter and engage the work of the Kingdom by one way only, which is through Jesus Christ (symbolic of the gate, entrance, and door). Finally, they are *evolutionary* in that they operate in full communion with God and are not resigned to the religious practices of the inner court or constrained by the dutiful obligations of the holy place.[18]

(5) The Spiritual Church

Jesus said, *"...upon this rock I will build my church; and the gates of hell shall not prevail against it."* (Mat. 16:18). Jesus held the position that His church was founded upon the revelation that He is (and forever will be) *"the Christ, the Son of the living God."* (Mat. 16:1617). Jesus had a very specific vision in mind when He established His Church. His vision entailed a body of people who were globally and universally connected. A people whose mission was so expansive that they could not be defined by a physical location or denomination.[19]

In the blog site, *Our Rabbi Jesus*, Tverberg offers insight into Jesus' claim to the title of *Christ*: "The title Christ comes from the Greek word *Christos* meaning anointed, [which is an] equivalent of the word *mashiach* or

Messiah in Hebrew. To be appointed such a title as *Christ* or *Messiah* is to suggest that the person is the anointed one of God. To be anointed, literally, is to have sacred oil poured on one's head, because God has chosen the person for a special task. Priests and kings were anointed, and occasionally prophets. Kings were anointed during their coronation rather than receiving a crown…Even though prophets and priests were anointed, the phrase "anointed one" or "the Lord's anointed" was most often used to refer to a king…The overriding biblical imagery of the word "Messiah" or "Christ" is that of a king chosen by God…The act of anointing with sacred oil emphasized that it was God himself who had ordained a person and given him authority to act as his representative." [Tverberg, 2016].

Paul later affirmed, through two separate admissions of his own, what Jesus initially declared: *"For no one can lay a foundation other than that which is laid, which is Jesus Christ"* (1 Cor. 3:11, ESV). *"God placed all things under his feet and appointed him to be head over everything for the church, which is his body, the fullness of him who fills everything in every way"* (Eph. 1:22-23, NIV). Paul appears to suggest here that Jesus established a new paradigm when it came to who and what the Church actually is and does.

Jesus established only one Church, which was comprised of a people like unto Himself. There is no evidence to support the idea that Jesus ever used the term "Christian" to describe His Church. The more appropriate term that more accurately describes the nature of His Church is the *Ecclesia.* That is to say, those *"called out of darkness"* and the world, into the *"marvelous light"* of Jesus Christ and God's Kingdom.[20] If Jesus alone has the authority to call, choose, and equip His Church, then He alone determines how each member will be used accordingly to build and further the work of His Kingdom. Hence, Paul's assertion: *"And he gave some, apostles; and some, prophets; and some, evangelists; and some, pastors and teachers; For the perfecting of the saints, for the work of the ministry, for the edifying of the body of Christ."* (Eph. 4:11-12).

(6) The Local Church

According to Act 11:26, the first local Christian assembly was established by a small group of believers in Antioch. They identified themselves as Christians to distinguish themselves as followers of Jesus Christ. It is unlikely that these early founders of the Christian church had anything in mind other than to further the gospel, employ the teachings of Jesus Christ, advance the Kingdom of God and adding *"to the church daily."* (Act 2:47).

A historical account of the Christian church as we know it today (with all its vestiges) is a far cry from what Jesus envisioned for the Church. In many ways, it has failed to be "house of prayer" and worship. (Mat. 21:13). Fundamentally, there is no question the local Christian church has value. However, given its doctrinal differences and divisions, one might go as far as to say it has lost its saltiness.[21] That is, it has failed to maintain the unity, singularity, and cohesiveness of the body of Christ; is often guilty of harboring bias towards women; has used the premise of faith to promote racial disparity and injustice; has encouraged a false sense of loyalty to a single person, institution, and/or religious organization for monetary gain; and has infamously fueled a continuance of infighting, confusion, and divisiveness that only serves to consistently divide the body of Christ.

As a result of its ambiguity, the "Christian church" has not only failed to produce viable candidates for service, but has largely disqualified them inasmuch as most are too immature and ill-equipped for the *"greater works"* of Jesus Christ. (John 14:12). As such, the Bible declares, *"...judgment [will] begin, starting with the house of God. And if it starts with us, what will be the fate of those who are disobedient to the gospel of God? And if the righteous are barely saved, what will become of the ungodly and sinners?"* (1 Pet. 4:17-18, NET). I contend, the only hope for the local Christian church today is for it to transform itself into the Church that Jesus envisioned and instituted.

(7) The Believer's Mandate

A "mandate" is defined as "an authoritative command, order, commission, or authorization to act, given to a representative." (Merriam-Webster.com (b), 2019). Our mandate as members of Christ's body is to speak, live and exemplify the Word of God in every aspect of life. We are His ambassadors and representatives on earth, carrying out our various assignments according to what He "commands, orders, commissions or authorizes," and not based on personal agenda.

Luke spells out in great detail what Jesus' thoughts and prayers were concerning the objectives of the Kingdom: *"...Thy kingdom come. Thy will be done, as in heaven, so in earth."* (Luke 11:2). Our Lord's greatest desire was that the will of the Father (the "Kingdom") be realized and manifested on earth, as it is in heaven. Jesus takes this analogy one step further through His metaphorical use of the word *seed* to explain the empirical influence of the Word of God on earth: *"The seed is the word of God."* (Luk. 8:11; Cp. Luk 8:12-15).

According to John, the Word of God *"was made flesh, and dwelt among us, (and we beheld his glory, the glory as of the only begotten of the Father), full of grace and truth."* (Joh. 1:14; Cp. Joh. 1:1-4). Based on this, Jesus Christ is the Word of God manifested in human form. Jesus, as the Word of God, demands five things of us:

1. Desire Him and mature as a result of His example.[22]
2. Study Him and do what He commands of us.[23]
3. Hear and receive Him, so we can bring forth fruit.[24]
4. Bear witness of His power and authenticity as God.[25]
5. Live, move, and have our being[26] in Him.

The believer's mandate then is governed and defined by our capacity to allow Jesus (the Word of God) to permeate our being and manifest Himself in and through us. To ignore this truth is to nullify any validity Jesus has in transforming us into His *"image"* and *"likeness."* (Gen. 1:26).

(8) The Law of Dominion

In the 2019 bio-drama *Harriet*, Cynthia Erivo (playing the iconic freedom fighter Harriet Tubman), strikes a blow against the atrocities of slavery through the statement, *"God don't mean people to own people!"* (Law, 2019). In the book of Genesis, our Creator (God) also addresses the subject in context of the word *dominion*.

The word *dominion* is a derivative from the Hebrew word *radah,* meaning to "have dominion over." Dominion directly relates to our mastery, excellence and influence in and on the earth as trusted guardians and caretakers of all that God created.[27] Certain fundamental laws apply when it comes to dominion. The principle law governing dominion is the ideology that human beings are not meant to exploit anything that God created, especially other human beings.

As it relates to dominion, Adam and Eve's first responsibility to God was to serve as trusted guardians and caretakers. God entrusted them with the responsibly of governing equitably, fairly, and impartially,[28] without discriminating or usurping power over other living beings or things. It is inherently wrong to promote one race over another or to tout slavery and human trafficking as a means of socio-economic empowerment. It is also inherently wrong to be divisive when it comes to ethnicity, culture, social status, the mistreatment of animals or the environment.

Jeremiah perfectly describes human nature when it comes to dominion: *"The heart is deceitful above all things, and desperately wicked: who can know it?"* (Jer. 17:9). In his countless writings on various Christian subjects, Andrew Basden insisted, "We have taken [the word *radah*] to mean dominate over just as a medieval ruler or potentate would dominate over his subjects, using them for his own ends, his own pleasure, his own prestige, his own wars, etc. But an examination of 'radah' shows that this is NOT the type of ‘dominion’ that we are called upon to have over the creation...our 'radah' of the creation is not to be with harshness, cruelty [or] selfishness...our 'radah' is not for our own sake, but for the sake of the one ruled, that is, for the sake of the creation. We should heal those parts of creation that are sick, bind up those parts that are injured, bring back those parts that are straying, search for those parts that have become lost...we radah creation to represent God to it, to develop and refine and beautify it for its own sake, rather than for ours. We are not to be destroyers nor consumers of the rest of creation, nor even stewards, but shepherds of the rest of creation.” (Basden, 2009).

The fact that we are so complicit in destroying life instead of preserving it is a clear indication that we have no real concept of what true dominion is. To understand dominion, one must understand God’s motives for endowing it in the first place: *“And God said, Let us make man in our image, after our likeness: and let them have dominion over the fish of the sea, and over the fowl of the air, and over the cattle, and over all the earth, and over every creeping thing that creepeth upon the earth.”* (Gen. 1:26).

The inference, *"let them have dominion,"* speaks to the responsibilities assigned to both the man and woman, respectively. It also suggests an equal partnership, ownership, and investment between men and women, irrespective of gender. In God's eyes, men and women are *different* when it comes to headship and gender, but equal when it comes to dominion, posterity, and heritage. This is an interesting concept to consider because it thoroughly dismantles any notion of a "male-dominated" society.

God's motives for endowing Adam and Eve with the gift of dominion was to formalize and secure their legacy, purpose and assignment as guardians and caretakers, from one generation to another. When they openly defied the authoritative command and will of God, they subsequently forfeited not only their rights to dominion, but also the rights of every generation to follow. The good news is, their disobedience led to a *"more excellent way,"*[29] which was fulfilled through Jesus Christ. He, in turn, set a precedence to show us the right way and use of dominion.

Had Adam and Eve fully embraced the vision God had for them, they most likely would have realized the Garden of Eden was merely a test run for what they would later govern on a global and universal scale, much like Jesus does now. Their inability to handle dominion responsibly also points to a serious flaw in the human nature. That is, when human ingenuity is employed outside the will of God, it results in some form of perversion, persecution, or disaster. As a countermeasure to these things, John advised the following:

"Do not love the world or the things in the world. If anyone loves the world, the love of the Father is not in him. For all that is in the world—the lust of the flesh, the lust of the eyes, and the pride of life—is not of the Father but is of the world. And the world is passing away, and the lust of it; but he who does the will of God abides forever." (1 Joh. 2: 15-17, NKJV).

Worldly dominion is self-centered and self-serving, being motivated by the *"desires of the flesh, desires of the eyes, and pride of life."* (1 Joh. 2:16). From these come the spirit of pride, greed, selfishness and physical/sexual cravings. The word *desire* or *lust* is derived from the Greek word *ephithymis*, meaning to have a strong "desire, craving, longing [or] desire for what is forbidden." (Blue Letter Bible Online, 2020).

Godly dominion is more altruistic in that it is God-centered and self-sacrificing, being motivated by the love of God, expressed through the Greek word *agápē*. Paul describes the nature of God's love in the following passage:

"Love is patient and kind; love does not envy or boast; it is not arrogant or rude. It does not insist on its own way; it is not irritable or resentful; it does not rejoice at wrongdoing but rejoices with the truth. Love bears all things, believes all things, hopes all things, endures all things." (1 Cor. 13:4-7, ESV).

(9) The Purpose of Unity

Unity is the foundation of all things. It is the basis of God's triune nature and the intimacy held between the Father, Son and Holy Spirit.[30] It was the premise behind Jesus choosing to wash His disciple's feet.[31] *"Peter saith unto Him, Thou shalt never wash my feet. Jesus answered him, If I wash thee not, thou hast no part with me. Simon Peter saith unto him, Lord, not my feet only, but also my hands and my head."* (Joh. 13:8-9). It was also the motive behind Paul's assertion, *"There is neither Jew nor Greek... bond nor free...male nor female: for ye are all one in Christ Jesus"* (Gal. 3:28).

Unity implies agreement and an integration of all things as one, working in complete harmony with the perfect will of God. Hence, Paul's assertion: *"There is one body, and one Spirit, even as ye are called in one hope of your calling; One Lord, one faith, one baptism, One God and Father of all, who is above all, and through all, and in you all."* (Eph. 4:4-6). Paul believed the Lord had a unique and uncanny way of unifying all things and causing them to fit together perfectly, especially when it came to His body of believers: *"We will speak the truth in love, growing in every way more and more like Christ, who is the head of his body, the church. He makes the whole body fit together perfectly. As each part does its own special work, it helps the other parts grow, so that the whole body is healthy and growing and full of love."* (Eph. 4:15-16, NLT).

(10) Built For Compatibility

"For as we have many members in one body, but all the members do not have the same function, so we, being many, are one body in Christ, and individually members of one another." (Rom. 12:4-5). The implications of unity are enormous when it comes to the body of Christ because we are built for compatibility, not comfort or convenience.

Compatibility, like unity, implies agreement, a common kinship, and like-mindedness. Hence, Paul's statement: *"If one part suffers, every part suffers with it; if one part is honored, every part rejoices with it."* (1 Cor. 12:26; Cp. 1 Cor. 12:21-25).

Comfort, on the other hand, implies an alleviation of discomfort, distress, turmoil, anxiety, grief, and pain. Jesus never promised that we would be free of such things. He said, *"If the world hates you, remember that it hated me first."* (Joh. 15:18, NIV).

Convenience involves a level of ease and satisfaction that is free of controversy, distraction, contention and resistance. Jesus never promised us a lifestyle free of controversy. However, He did say, I have told you these things, so that in me you may have peace. In this world you will have trouble. But take heart! I have overcome the world." (Joh. 16:33, NIV).

(11) Wholeness in Christ

One final discipline, which I found to be of great benefit is wholeness in Christ. Paul viewed *wholeness* in terms of *sanctification: "And the very God of peace sanctify you wholly; and I pray God your whole spirit and soul and body be preserved blameless unto the coming of our Lord Jesus Christ."* (1 Thes. 5:23). In other words, Paul believed every believer should present their body as *"living sacrifice, holy [and] acceptable unto God."* (Rom. 12:1).

James, the half-brother of Jesus, considered *wholeness* as a lifelong process designed to draw out certain godly attributes in believers: *"Consider it pure joy, my brothers and sisters, whenever you face trials of many kinds, because you know that the testing of your faith produces perseverance [or patience]. Let perseverance [or patience] finish its work so that you may be mature and complete, not lacking anything."* (Jam. 1:2-4, NIV).

Moreover, James viewed *wholeness* in terms of striving to be both *perfect* and *complete* in Christ. To be made perfect (or otherwise whole), a believer would need to come into a place of spiritually maturity such that he/ she is equipped with the fundamental attributes required to fulfill one's calling, assignment, and purpose in life. We can easily determine the validity of James' thought process by deconstructing the words sanctify, perfect, and complete.

The word *sanctify* is derived from the Greek word *hagiazō*, which has a double meaning. It can mean to be honored ("hallowed") for one's lifestyle in choosing to be separated from secular things and completely dedicated to God. It can also mean to be highly respected ("venerable") for one's wisdom, knowledge, experience, and righteous character. (Strong's G37, 2020).

The word *perfect* is derived from the Greek word *teleios,* meaning to come of age and full maturity, such that one exhibits the highest level of human integrity, virtue, and skill. (Strong's G5046, 2020). Finally, the word c*omplete* is derived from the Greek word *holoklēros,* meaning to become so sound in body, soul, and spirit that one becomes ethically faultless. (Strong's G3648, 2020).

(12) Our Triune Nature

During the 1988 NAACP Image Awards, Luther Vandross famously performed one Dionne Warwick's most successful singles, *A House Is Not A Home*. (Genius Media Group, Inc., 2020). One might argue, from a psychological standpoint, that the lyrics of the song are expressing the difference between human interaction and affection versus that of an intangible object. The rational of the lyrics is "a house is not a home" without intimacy and interconnectedness within the house.

The same might be said of the relationship shared between our triune nature, consisting of body, soul and spirit. The human body, soul and spirit are not intangible objects void of relationship to one another. They are, in fact, interconnected to one another and play an essential part in who we are and what makes us uniquely different from one another as created beings.[32]

If we truly revered our *body* as a holy sanctuary and habitation for God, then we would not be so quick to abuse or mistreat it. We would instead cherish and honor it, caring for both its interior and exterior maintenance. Moreover, if we truly revered our *soul* and *spirit,* then we take great care in guarding them both, to assure that nothing infiltrated or contaminated our relationship with God. We would instead do everything in our power to create a peaceful, sanctified habitation for the Holy Spirit to dwell in to commune with us. And we would avoid any short-term or long-term psychological or spiritual[33] damage by studiously taking into account our fundamental nature. *Watchman Nee*,[34] a profound leader, teacher, and seer of divine revelation, speaks extensively about the triune nature of man in his book, *The Spiritual Man.*

The Body. The body of man has world-consciousness in that it "affects" and is "affected by" the sensuous and material aspects of the world. The only thing restraining the body is the spirit of man, for only "the spirit can subdue the body, through the medium of the soul, to make it obey God." In contrast, "the body, through the soul, can [also] draw the spirit into loving the world." (Nee (a), 1977). Given the body's inclination to engage the world, Paul proposed: *"present your bodies a living sacrifice, holy, acceptable unto God, which is your reasonable service."* (Rom. 12:1). Simply put, the sanctity of the body greatly depends on our ability to revere it as a holy sanctuary, dedicated unto God.

The Soul. The soul of man has "self-consciousness" in that it is the seat of the will (what I want), emotions (what I feel), and the intellect (what I think). It is the part of our triune nature that operates according to freewill and serves as a medium for the human ego and personality. The soul is "the meeting point of spirit and body." It stands between and belongs to the "two worlds" of the body and spirit. "It is linked with the spiritual world through the spirit and with the material world through the body." It is of great significance to us because it is the place where the "spirit and body are merged," to regulate "man's personality and influence." Originally, "before man committed sin, the power of the soul was under the dominion of the spirit. Its strength was therefore the spirit's strength. The spirit itself cannot act upon the body. It can only do so through the medium of the soul." (Nee (a), 1977).

Ezekiel the Prophet insisted, *"The soul that sinneth, it shall die."* (Eze. 18:4, 20). Sin is not some ambiguous or arbitrary concept. It is the equivalent of anarchy: The willful intent to either usurp (assume unjust rule, dominion or authority) and/or openly defy (resist or refuse to obey) the authoritative command and will of God. (OED (a-b), 2019). Because the soul's natural inclination is to sin, it must be regenerated (born again)[35] by the Spirit of God before it can enter into a place of communion with God. As such, one of many assignments tasked to the Holy Spirit[36] is to clean, repair and restore the soul to its original state, which is in full communion with God.

The Spirit. The spirit of man has God-consciousness in that it is created to be the habitation and dwelling place of the Holy Spirit. (Nee (a), 1977). The Bible contends, *"God is a Spirit: and they that worship him must worship him in spirit and in truth."* (Joh. 4:24). Recognizing the work of the Holy Spirit after new birth, Nee states, "we must next observe exactly where He does dwell… *"Do you not know that you are God's temple and that God's Spirit dwells in you?"* (1 Cor. 3:16)…the Dweller and his dwelling must share the same character. Only man's regenerated spirit—not the mind, emotion or volition of his soul [nor] his body—is fit to be God's dwelling place. The Spirit is both a builder and a dweller. He cannot dwell where He has not built: He builds to dwell and dwells only in what He has built." (Nee (b), 1977).

Nee goes on to state, "The human spirit is said to be comprised of three parts…the conscience, intuition and communion. The conscience is the discerning organ which distinguishes right and wrong; not as a consequence of knowledge stored in the mind but rather by a spontaneous [conscience] judgment. The work of the conscience is independent and direct [in that] it does not bend to outside opinions…The intuition is the sensing organ of the human spirit. It is so diametrically different from physical sense and soulish sense that it is called intuition. Intuition involves a direct sensing independent of any outside influence. Communion is worshiping God. God is not apprehended by our thoughts, feelings or intentions, for He can only be known directly in our spirits." (Nee (c), 1977).

CHAPTER THREE

THE REVELATION

1962 was a pivotal year for me personally and spiritually. It was the year my brother was born and I gained a life-long friend and sibling; the year my dad officially retired from the military after 20 years of service; the year our family moved from Vicenza, Italy to the Black community of Newtown in Elkton, Virginia; and the year I was formally introduced to my maternal side of the family, the Toliver's.

What fascinated me about my maternal grandparents, (Silas and Edith Toliver) was the veracity in which they lived: Undaunted by the lack of modern conveniences, they lived as if they had no want or need for anything. They seemed to possess a type of wealth that had no apparent ties to money. Water for drinking, cooking, and bathing was drawn from a cistern outside the home and carried into the house by the bucket full. All meals were prepared over a wood-burning cast-iron stove and enjoyed in the company of family, and occasionally a few friends. There were no thermostats to regulate the temperature inside the house. In the Winter, heat was generated by shoveling coal into a furnace twice a day. In the Summer, we cooled ourselves by the shade created on my grandparent's front porch, as we sat around snapping peas or string beans. Everyone, including myself, was resigned to using an outhouse by day and a portable chamber pot at night.

By today's standards, my grandparent's lifestyle might sound crude and unrefined. But in the mind of an impressionable nine-year-old, who had never experienced anything like this before, it was a quick study in simplicity and learning how to adjust to change. It was one of many fond memories of my maternal grandparents that has been deeply woven and ingrained into the threads of my personality. Memories that later in life would serve me well as I transitioned from a state of adolescence to adulthood.

* * *

Surrendering to adulthood is not an easy process by any stretch of the imagination. Still, it is vital that we mature and come into adulthood, if for no other reason than to be an asset to the generations that follow. As adults, we often make the mistake of thinking that adulthood is synonymous with maturity, or that it can be defined by age, intelligence, knowledge, or skill. In truth, the process of maturity is something that begins at birth and continues throughout life. So, to naively think *maturity* is a fluid process, absent of highs, lows, mountain top, and valley experiences is a misnomer—a false and misleading conclusion.

Paul had a very interesting perspective when it came to adulthood and spiritual maturity. Regarding adulthood, he considered a person to be an adult when they reached the age of accountability, that is, when they could reasonably be held accountable for their actions. He believed, once accountable, every adult also bore the responsibility of exhibiting some level of maturity, equivalent to their age and acquisition of wisdom. Paul's stance position on the subject was so poignant that he held himself accountable:

"When I was a child, I [spoke] as a child, I understood as a child, I thought as a child: but when I became a man, I put away childish things." (1 Cor. 13:11).

Paul's perception of spiritual maturity was equally insightful. In contrast to adulthood, Paul considered spiritual maturity to be the *"prize"* one acquired as a result of the pursuit of *"the high calling of God in Christ Jesus."* (Phil. 3:14). In turn, the *high calling* was a matter of aspiring to become a mirror image of Jesus Christ, as it relates to His nature, character, and behavior. Hence, Paul's statement:

"Now we see things imperfectly, like puzzling reflections in a mirror, but then we will see everything with perfect clarity. All that I know now is partial and incomplete, but then I will know everything completely, just as God now knows me completely." (1 Cor. 13:12, NLT).

A Call to Maturity

I personally never gave much thought to spiritual maturity until the Lord challenged my perceptions of it in a very unorthodox way. Routinely, around 3:00 a.m. every morning, the Lord would have the Holy Spirit nudge me in the spirit to wake me up so I could begin my daily regimen of writing. Like a child, I would murmur and complain, roll over, and fall back to sleep. To be perfectly honest, I was a bit annoyed by these early morning wake-up calls. After all, what possible motive could the Lord have for choosing to wake me up at such an ungodly hour when He could have easily picked another time when I was fully awake?

As it turns out, the Lord had a very good reason for waking me up so early, none of which had anything to do with a personal intrusion of my time or feelings. In reality, I was being trained and groomed for my future engagement as a writer. A necessary qualification to carry out the assignment was in learning how to be sensitive and immediately responsive to the Lord's voice whenever He was speaking. Him waking me up early in the morning was simply discipline designed to equip me as a writer.

My wanton disregard of His early morning wakeup calls not only proved that I was spiritually immature, but also not disciplined enough to handle the assignment He was preparing me for. To flush out and modify my behavior, the Lord employed another disciplinary action and tactic: One night while lying in bed, I heard a majestic song being sung by an angelic choir. The chords, melody, and words were so unbelievably simple, I was convinced I would remember everything the next morning. Of course, the next morning I remembered nothing, not even melody or lyrics. I was so heartbroken over having missed a part of God that I vowed never to pass up another opportunity to commune with God on His terms.

Not long after this first experience, the Lord began to talk about His dealing with us at different stages of life. The two lessons, which occurred on two consecutive Saturdays, dramatically changed my perspective of spiritual maturity and adulthood:

SATURDAY, JUNE 18, 2005

I received my usual wake-up call from the Holy Spirit to get up and begin writing. I remember wanting to sleep in late that morning but could sense the Lord had something important to share. Before I could get one leg out of the bed and drag myself downstairs to get on the computer, the Holy Spirit began to speak:

"At some point the breastfeeding and spoon feeding has got to stop." He said.

I abruptly sat up in bed, expecting to hear more but there was nothing more. Feeling a bit confused and baffled, I thought, *"What the heck does that mean?"* Although I did not understand the meaning behind what He was saying, I had enough sense at this point to not question Him. So, I obediently got up, washed my face, and immediately made my way downstairs. It took several days to unpack the meaning behind His words but I eventually came into the understanding that He wanted to address the issues of spiritual infancy and adolescence.

Spiritual Infancy

Naturally speaking, all newborns are considered innocent in that they have no concept of right and wrong, or good and evil. They are incapable of digesting solid foods and must derive their primary source of nutrition from breast feeding and milk. Their whole purpose for living is defined and determined through the relationship they share with their mother. A good mother suffers the agony and pain of labor, to successfully birth her baby into the world. As the baby's primary caregiver, she is responsible for carrying the baby to term. After the baby's birth, she continues to invest in the longevity of her child, influencing not only its personality but its socialization into the world.

Spiritually speaking, the same can be said of spiritual newborns, that is, those who are born again[37] and qualify as spiritual infants.[38] Similar to their natural counterparts, spiritual newborns are incapable of digesting meat[39] (the Word in its revelatory form) and, therefore, must derive their primary source of nutrition from breast feeding and the milk of the Word.

Their purpose and identity are defined and determined as a result of their relationship with Jesus Christ. As their sole Provider, Life-giver,[40] and Caretaker, Jesus takes on the persona of a mother in a number of ways: He carries His babies to full in the sense that He is sensitive to their needs, and intimately involved in their lives. During this phase of their development, He nurtures them and continuously feeds them. His is extremely affectionate and pampering. He provides a sense of comfort, warmth, and protection. He is quick to respond to their needs when they are in distress, frequently coddling them with unexpected blessings to comfort and console them.

Given the Lord's tendency to be extremely forgiving and accommodating during this phase of spiritual growth, spiritual newborns often misinterpret His actions as extreme favor. As such, in public, they present as overly zealous and extremely preachy, often to a fault. When in reality, they should utilize this time of intimacy to develop a close bond with their Caregiver.

So, when the Lord said, "at some point, the breastfeeding has got to stop," it was His way of telling me that I was no longer spiritual baby that required coddling and breast-feeding.

Spiritual Adolescence

It is common knowledge that the adolescent years are tumultuous, filled with a great deal of anxiety and frustration on the part of teenagers or adolescents. Psychology Today, describes this "transitional stage as a time of disorientation and discovery…that period of time when an adolescent "raises questions of independence and identity…cultivate their sense of self, [and] face difficult choices about academics, friendship, sexuality, gender, identity, drugs, and alcohol." The article goes onto say, "most teens have a relatively egocentric perspective on life" in the sense that they "often focus on themselves and believe that everyone else…is focused on them too." (Psychology Today, 2020).

Spiritual adolescence can be a very tumultuous and anxious period of time. Most spiritual adolescents are unlearned and unstable[41] when it comes to their knowledge of God and, therefore, must be taught. Influenced greatly by the ease of their former state as *newly born infants*, they are easily prone to throwing temper tantrums when they do not get their way; or when the Lord does not immediately respond to their requests (prayers) as expected. They are seemingly unaware that the world does not revolve around them solely and/or that the Lord dealings are not limited to their needs alone.

Individuals who are in a state of *spiritual adolescence* are easily prone to impatience, ill-tempered ways and naivety. They are often indecisive when it comes to choosing between right and wrong, good and evil, and/or purpose and intent. Their willful disregard of sound counsel and instruction places them in a unique category of individuals who are defined as being easily deceived and led astray.[42] They are often guilty of misinterpreting Scripture to suit their own situations, and are quick to find fault in others but rarely in themselves.

Rather than develop an intimate relationship with Jesus Christ, many spiritual adolescents rely heavily on the local church as their primary source of fulfillment. The Bible likens them to those who are carnal,[43] lukewarm,[44] and given to all sorts of unnatural affections.[45] They are too immature to live solely off the *meat*[46] of the Word, and thus, can only sustain a diet of milk[47] and bread.[48]

The Lord's interaction with spiritual adolescents is generally disciplinary in relationship. As such, He frequently finds it necessary to establish boundaries to teach and encourage corrective behavior. Though His approach may seem unduly harsh and unfair at times, His grace suggests otherwise, for He is forever loving, kind and merciful to all with equal impunity. What most spiritual adolescents fail to recognize is whatever form of disciplinary action the Lord may choose to impose upon them, it is not meant to be abusive or dismissive, but rather corrective and educational. His goal is not to instill fear, exact punishment, or promote retribution, but to encourage corrective behavior so the individual can *"grow up into him in all things."* (Eph. 4:15).

So, when the Lord said, "at some point, the spoon-feeding has got to stop," it was His way of telling me that it was time to stop acting like a spiritual adolescent in the sense of demanding to be spoon-fed all the answers all the time, and easily prone to emotional breakdowns and temper tantrums. The time had come for me to grow up and measure myself against "the stature of the fullness of Christ." (Eph. 4:13).

SATURDAY, JUNE 25, 2005

The following Saturday, I was awakened again by the Holy Spirit to begin my daily regime of writing. I had not slept well the night before, worried over a new job I had accepted and now wanted out of. After being laid off from my previous job, a new opportunity had quickly open for me in less than a month. I was excited about the new opportunity but after a week or so, discovered my new employer had been less than honest in their business dealings and offerings. I did not want to appear ungrateful to the Lord for the provision, but it put me in a tough spot, trying to decide whether stay or leave.

"Maybe a mindless, non-challenging job is exactly what I need at this point in life," I thought to myself, *"after all, I am no spring chicken and no longer at the prime of my career."*

Somehow, that rational did not make a lot of sense to me. Settling was an easier choice to make because it required no effort on my part, but I was tired of being stuck in some endless cycle of always settling for less than God's best. Looking for another job was definitely an option, but it meant re-entering the job market. Frankly, I was tired of putting on a game face and jumping through hoops, just to prove to some employer I would be an asset to their company. Plus, if I looked for another job, there were no guarantees when or if I would find one.

Every time I would weigh my options, a knot would curl up in my stomach. I felt as though I was being held hostage in my own mind, by a set of circumstances I never asked for or wanted. With so many unforeseen variables at stake, the anxiety of not knowing what to do or which way to turn conjured up feelings of guilt and frustration.

I could feel the Lord tugging at my soul and spirit to not give in to such a meager existence, but I did not have the patience to wait on Him. I wanted (needed) an immediate solution to my situation. The struggle taking place inside me got so real at times that the slightest hint of someone asking me about the job would elicit a knee-jerk reaction:

"I am struggling with this job! Can you please pray for me! I am struggling with this job!" I would plead.

I remember the puzzled looks on people's faces as they tried to figure out who this crazy person was standing in front of them. No one was more aware of how insane I sounded than me. So, on this particular Saturday morning, I thought it best that I spend some time in prayer:

"Lord, I am really struggling with this job and I really need your guidance on whether to leave, stay, or just rest," I prayed softly.

"When are you going to stop struggling and learn to walk with me?" the Lord replied.

I immediately sat up in bed, feeling as though someone had thrown a bucket of ice-cold water in my face. I had unknowingly allowed the word *struggle* to permeate all my thoughts, conversations, and prayers. There was no question the struggle was real at times, but the question I had to ask myself was: "If I am still struggling with things, am I truly resting and trusting in God by faith? The answer was no. If I had not learned to enter into God's rest, then clearly I still had some growing up to do.

The Struggle

As adults, we struggle with just about everything. We struggle with our jobs, identity, and relevance in the church and society. We struggle in our relationships with our spouses, children, siblings, family members, and friends. We struggle with what to eat or not eat, what to wear or not wear. We struggle with how much money we make, whether we need more money or worry that we do not make enough to sustain us. We struggle with how we look and whether our attractiveness measures up to the standards of others. We struggle with being too fat or too thin. The question the Lord posed to me is the question He asks of us all.

The thing about spiritual maturity is it requires both transformation and alignment. It requires transformation in that our minds must be renewed daily.[49] Renewing the mind daily requires that we seek Him daily for guidance and instruction. It also requires that we level up to maturity, such that we no longer need to be breast-fed like a baby or spoon-fed like a child. Instead, we must be mature enough to allow the Lord to guide us *"into all truth."* (Joh. 16:13).

Spiritual maturity also requires alignment in the sense that we are no longer to be guided by our sensibilities and will, but rather subject and submitted to God's perfect and divine will. Aligning oneself with the will of God requires that we grow up and accept responsibility for our own actions, behavior, and failures in life. It will force us to stop playing the role of a victim, viewing ourselves as a victims of circumstance, and/or habitually blaming others for our own shortcomings, misgivings, and failures.

Spiritual Adulthood

The transition between spiritual adolescence and spiritual adulthood can be a confusing and challenging time of social change, demands, and expectations. Some adults find this experience to be so challenging that they often live in denial of it, often reverting to previous stages of development in an attempt to cope. This is due, in part, to mature leaders, advisers, and counselors not addressing issues of immaturity when they first encounter it.

During this phase of maturation, the Lord often takes a hands-off approach in dealing with us as adults. He may at times appear distant, unresponsive, nonchalant, or even dismissive when it comes to our prayers and needs. When He does speak, He rarely offers any explanation for the delay. Instead, He expects complete obedience and compliance to His directives, without question, hesitation or complaint. His reasoning for interacting with us in this manner has a lot to do with accountability and responsibility.

Psalm 23:5 says, *"Thou preparest a table before me in the presence of mine enemies..."* If Jesus has prepared a table in the presence of my enemies, then my enemies are no threat to me. They are, at best, merely spectators, onlookers, and observers of the blessings and provisions the Lord has prepared before me. Furthermore, if my every need, want, or desire has already been prepared, then whatever portion has been allotted to me already exists and is mine for the taking. I do not need to beg, plead, or lament for something that already belongs to me. All I really need to do is pull up a chair to the Lord's table and begin feasting off the blessings of God. Here is another thing to consider.

When it comes to prayer specifically, the Bible says, we are not to pray in *"vain repetitions as the heathen do,"* but rather to ask the Lord to *"give us our daily bread."* (Matt. 6:7). Asking for our *daily bread* is the equivalent of asking for our daily portion. Whatever portion the Lord chooses to give us, His expectation is always based on a return, that we would maximize our portion for potential increase and fruitfulness. (Mat. 13:23).

Consequently, when the Lord invites us to His table, we are not His guests. We are members of His family. No well-intentioned family member would ever wait to be asked to take a seat at the table, to dine with other family members. To the contrary, it is a forgone thought that once the table is set and all is prepared, every family member gathers around the table and takes their respective seats.

Knowing we have a seat at the table and can participant in the Lord's blessings should be enough to sustain us. We should never worry over what blessings are for us (or when/ if we will receive them) because Jesus promised, *"No good thing will [I] withhold from them that walk uprightly."* (Psa. 84:11). He also said, *"If ye then, being evil, know how to give good gifts unto your children, how much more shall your Father which is in heaven give good things to them that ask him?"* (Mat. 7:11; Cp. Luk. 11:13).

Jesus' response to our needs, wants, and desires tells us several things: One, whatever I need, want, or desire I have, both now and in the future, has already been prepared and provided for me. Two, whatever provision or allotment the Lord gives us is always subject to the will of the Father, and based on His timing, season and desires.

Our greatest desire should be to come into a place of spiritual maturity and adulthood. So then, when the Lord asked the question, "when are you going to stop struggling and learn to walk with me," what He was trying to tell me is to grow up and mature into a place where I know who I am, and what position I hold as a member of His family.

The Necessity of Maturity

Spiritual maturity is both a rite of passage and privilege. The fact that we are granted this privilege every day is a gift, and one we should be eternally thankful for. Nothing can prevent us from becoming spiritually mature unless we choose to believe we do not need it or are not worthy of it. None of us should ever fall into a state of complacency, such that we are unable or unwilling to grow. Paul described this state of mind perfectly: *"You have been believers so long now that you ought to be teaching others. Instead, you need someone to teach you again the basic things about God's word. You are like babies who need milk and cannot eat solid food."* (Heb. 5:12, NLT).

When the Lord speaks, His words are always concise, timely, accurate and intentional. When it comes to salvation and deliverance, He says, *"hear me."*[50] When it comes to submission and obedience, He says, *"obey me."*[51] When it comes to discipleship and stewardship, He says, *"follow me."*[52] The qualifier for hearing, obeying, and following Christ is marked by three things: One, our ability to *spiritually discern* (perceive, recognize, be keenly aware of) the things of God; two, our ability to hear the Word, understand it, and *be fruitful*; and three, our ability to progressively *mature* into the image and likeness of Christ.

When combined, spiritual discernment, fruitfulness, and maturity become the basis for differentiating between those who do "good works" versus those who do "greater works."[53] Matthew explained it this way, *"Be ye therefore perfect, even as your Father which is in heaven is perfect."* (Mat. 5:48). To be *perfect* does not mean to be faultless, flawlessness, or guiltless. It simply means that a person has acquired a sense of wholeness, completeness, and excellence in Christ.[54]

Here is how Paul explained it. He said, *"Solid food [strong meat] is for the mature, for those who have their powers of discernment trained by constant practice to distinguish good from evil."* (Heb. 5:14, ESV). The ability to digest solid food (or strong meat) simply means that a person is mature and spiritually discerning enough to comprehend and interpret the revelatory things of God. It implies that a person's spiritual senses have been refined and fine-tuned to distinguish between good and evil, right and wrong, righteousness and unrighteousness. Therefore, when confronted with evil or someone who falsely claims to be an instrument of God,[55] the person is not so easily swayed, taken in, or deceived.

CHAPTER FOUR

THE ENCOUNTER

The date was July 20, 1969. I remember the occasion well because Apollo 11 had made its mark in history with the first successful American-manned mission and landing on the moon. All the media outlets were in a frenzy, televising Neil Armstrong's first man-made footprint on the moon, along with Edwin "Buzz" Aldrin bouncing around on the moon. Landing on the moon was a big deal for the United States in those days, not only because it was a historical event ("one small step for man") but also because it was an extraordinary feat ("one giant leap for mankind").[56]

* * *

The Apollo 11 mission was the most talked about event of that decade. However, it paled in comparison to the experience of me growing up in the Shenandoah Valley, listening to the stories of my maternal and paternal grandparents. Both sides of my families had migrated from other surrounding counties to put down stakes in the newly formed community of Newtown. According to my paternal side of the family, the Walkers, Newtown was a densely wooded area at the onset of its development and populated primarily by American Indians and People of Color. The family would often swamp stories about Granddaddy Ananias and how he walked the distance between Stanardsville, Virginia (Rt. 29) and East Elkton (Rt. 33)—scaling the length of the Blue Ridge Mountains—for work every day. He did so with such grace, humility, and tenacity that it was almost sounded too surreal to be true. We all knew that Granddaddy Ananias was a man of integrity and great character. When it came to providing for his family or purchasing one and a half acres of land in Newtown, no sacrifice was too great.

There was something about stories like this that caused me to have a deep respect and admiration for paternal grandparents, Ananias and Annie R. Walker. In the short time that I was fortunate to have them in my life, I never knew them to be anything other than kind, generous, and loving in nature. As it turns out, the Apollo 11 mission and my paternal grandparents were not the only topics of discussion that year. Another amazing event was about to take place in the late Summer/early Fall of 1969, which would overshadow them both.

I was 15 years old that Summer. My brother, Ralph ("Dante"), was 6, and my first cousin, Timothy ("Timmy") from Philadelphia, PA, was 9. Timmy had come down for the Summer to hang out with my brother, while staying with Nanna, my paternal grandmother, who lived a stone's throw away from our modest little mobile home which sat on her property. On the day in question, there were no adults around to supervise the three of us. My dad, who was now fully retired from the military, worked in nearby Washington, D.C. during the week and on some weekends. My mom was at work in nearby Harrisonburg, VA, where she worked as a blue-collar worker. Nanna had left briefly to run a few errands in downtown Elkton, VA, leaving me in charge of two mischievous little boys.

My Divine Encounter

My best guess is the divine encounter took place sometime around late July or early August of 1969, as it occurred not long after the Apollo 11 mission to the moon. I had prepared a quick lunch for the three of us that afternoon. Before I could blink an eye, Dante and Timmy had gobbled up their food and were already outside horsing around. After clearing the table and washing the dishes, I decided to join them outside. There was something unusual about this particular day. I remember thinking how perfect the day seemed—not too cold or hot—with a warm breeze stirring the air. The clouds appeared brilliantly white and fluffy, and the sun appeared more radiant than I ever recall noticing before. I shrugged my shoulders resigning the whole matter as a figment of my imagination and continued watching Dante and Timmy horsing around with each other.

"Look at that!" Dante yelled, pointing towards the sky.

Timmy and I stopped dead in our tracks, looking in the direction he was pointing. There before our very eyes, was a full body image of Jesus Christ made entirely out of clouds! His arms were stretched wide open as if welcoming us into the comfort of His arms. I remember being mesmerized by the detail of His clothing, hands, and feet. Unlike His hands and articles of clothing, His face was indistinguishable, as if to suggest that His physical features were of no real importance.

His hair was shoulder length and wavy. Every aspect of His garments, which consisted of a full length tunic and sash tied around his waist, was brilliant white in color. Even more remarkable was His face, hands, and feet, which appeared darker in coloration from the rest of His garments. In the center of both hands and feet were darker spots, as if to confirm the legitimacy of His crucifixion. I remember thinking how similar in appearance He was to the photograph in our family Bible, but with one exception: This Jesus was distinctively a man of color and not Caucasian.

Wide-eyed with amazement, we continued watching as the image of Christ (made entirely from clouds) began to slowly dissipate. Shortly thereafter, other images appeared to His right (our left) of where His image first appeared. Representing the past, we saw images of Mary and Joseph with the baby Jesus, Noah's Ark, and other biblical characters which I no longer recall. Each image would appear briefly and then slowly dissipate, before another one would appear. When all these events had ended, a perfect replica of the first man-made footprint on the moon appear on His left (our right), representing the present. Not fully comprehending the magnitude of what we had just witnessed, the three of us stood motionless and speechless.

"God surely sees and knows all things," I thought privately.

We had witnessed something so incomprehensible that it was difficult to wrap our minds around it. Thinking this was the end of it all, the three of us just stared at each other, trying to process what we had just seen and experienced.

"Look at that arrow!" Timmy yelled.

Dante and I turned around almost in unison. Nearly 180 degrees from our original vantage point, appeared a perfect image of an arrow made entirely out of clouds, pointing towards (what we were told was) the North. I remember thinking how this might be a sign from the Lord, telling us either where to go, or where to look for His appearance at His second coming. As the arrow slowly dissipated, the three of us stood frozen in place, mesmerized by all the events we had witnessed on that day. Suddenly, the reality of all that had occurred finally hit us: Of all the people in the world, the Lord chose the three of us to bear witness to this extraordinary event.

The sheer thought of knowing we were chosen by God made us giddy with joy. We started laughing and hugging each other, as tears of joy ran down our faces. It was an indescribable moment for the three of us, and one that will remain an important memory forever.

As for me personally, it solidified in my mind that Jesus Christ is not some fictional character conjured up in the minds of men. He is everything the Father and the Bible proclaims Him to be,[57] and so much more. Most of all, it satisfied for me the question of what He looks like. From that day forward, I would never again accept the possibility of the Son of God being anything other than a man of color.

The Testimony

"Nana, Nana!! Guess what we saw!" we shouted, as we rushed towards her like defensive football team.

"Oh, y'all ain't seen no such a thing!" Nana replied.

"Y'all probably just saw some clouds that looked like some images!"

"No, Nanna, really! We really did see all those images," we responded in unison.

We tried relentlessly to convince Nanna that something extraordinary had happened to us, but she refused to believe us. Instead, she discarded the whole matter as the foolish ramblings of three imaginary minds. We were deeply hurt that she did not believe us but determined not to allow her or anyone else to dismiss the matter as something imaginary.

When my mom arrived home from work several hours later, we surrounded her reciting the entire incident again, with little thought to how tired she might be from having worked all day. We watched her facial expressions, waiting on a response, but she just stared at us seemingly at a loss for words.

"Are you sure you didn't see some clouds that looked like the image of Christ in the sky?" she inquired.

"No, we really did see it!" the three of us responded.

My mother did not know what to make of our claims. She knew we were not prone to making up outlandish stories, but it sounded too impossible to be true. Without further discussion, she ushered us into the house. No matter how incredible it may have sounded, we knew the truth and no amount of doubt on the part of the adults in our lives was going to convince us otherwise. Now, if only there was some way to prove that what we saw was not a figment of our imagination.

The Confirmation

The next morning my mother, brother, and I were sitting at the kitchen table having breakfast, when there was a sudden loud knocking at the door. Wide-eyed and slightly out of breath, Nanna came rushing through the door:

"Annie V, you know them children weren't lying after all! I was listening to my morning talk show on the radio and a lady called in wanting to know if anyone had seen those images in the sky yesterday! Oh, Lord, I can't believe it!" Nanna exclaimed, as she collapsed into the chair.

"Bebe, you should call the radio station and tell them what you saw!" Nanna said.

Shocked that my grandmother would expose me to public humiliation, I stood frozen in place.

"Uh un, I ain't calling nobody! People round here will think I'm crazy!" I responded.

"Oh, ain't nothing to be ashamed of girl! Call the radio station!" Nana insisted.

"You really should think about calling them, Bebe," my mother chimed in softly.

"Uh un, I ain't calling nobody!" I protested.

"Why can't one of you call them!"

Regretfully, I never made the call to the radio station on that day. I often think of the countless souls that might have come to Christ if I had only had the courage to speak up. At the very least, I should have validated the woman on the radio, if for no other reason than to put her mind at ease. But I was young and too fearful of being scrutinized and criticized in the public's eye to exhibit any sense of bravery or loyalty on that day.

Like Peter, I became an unsuspecting victim of my own fears and fragility; and yet, an willing participant in a life lesson that would transform my life. When put to the test, I had failed miserably to be witness for Christ. Because of it, I learned an important life lesson that day: Sometimes it is not enough to believe and acknowledge Christ. The day will surely come when we must take a stance in our confession of Christ: *"Whosoever therefore shall confess Me [Jesus] before men, him will I confess also before my Father which is in heaven."* (Mat. 10:32).

As Paul so eloquently put it, *"For I am not ashamed of the gospel of Christ: for it is the power of God unto salvation to everyone that believeth; to the Jew first, and also to the Greek."* (Rom. 1:16).

CHAPTER FIVE

THE PATH

One of my all-time favorite movies is the blockbuster film, The Matrix. In the first installment of the film, Morpheus tells Neo that he is the one—the one who's purpose is inexplicably tied to the survival of Zion. Neo is then given a choice, "Take the blue pill and the story ends, and you wake up in your bed believing whatever you want to believe," or "take the red pill and stay in wonderland, and I will show you how deep the rabbit hole goes." (YouTube, 2013).

* * *

Like many of us, Neo struggled with the idea of being a chosen vessel of divine purpose. Everything he believed in up to that point was based on the familiar, what he could control, and all the things that made him feel comfortable and safe. He could not fathom the idea of becoming the one because it disrupted his sensibilities and perceptions of life. When Morpheus called him to task, requiring him to step outside his comfort zone, he suddenly questions his potential. Neo is too cowardly to accept Morpheus' challenge at face value because he believes himself to be too insignificant, unworthy, and under qualified for such a profound assignment. And yet, he is too curiously courageous to not entertain the possibility of it. He questions whether he can live up to the expectations placed upon him; or carry the weight of the burden of all those who look up to him. Morpheus (like Jesus) is keenly aware of Neo's mental conflict and confused state of mind. To put Neo's mind at ease, and offer him some comfort, Morpheus proposes that there is a difference between knowing the path and actually walking it.

Knowing vs. Walking

Matthew does not mince words when it comes to pointing out the difference between knowing the path and walking it. According to Matthew, there are only two paths in life one may take: The road that leads to *life* or the road that leads to *destruction*: *"Enter through the narrow gate. For wide is the gate and broad is the road that leads to destruction, and many enter through it. But small is the gate and narrow the road that leads to life, and only a few find it."* (Mat. 7:13-14, NIV).

In this particular passage, Matthew goes on to describe the nature of the two paths, as well as those who choose to walk them. He says, *"many enter through"* the gate that leads to the road to destruction, for the gate is wide and broad, and open to anyone; but *"only a few find"* the road that leads to life, for the gate thereof is small and narrow, and open only to *"God's elect."*[58]

Notice Matthew's intentional phrasing of *"many enter through"* versus *"only a few find."* The fact that only a few find the road to life is not an opinion, it is a fact of life.[59] The reality is, the path to life is often burdensome and riddled with insurmountable odds, crisis, and undue hardships. There is no escaping the realities of this path because it comes par for the course. Jesus is not insensitive to all the challenges we face, for He has experienced[60] and endured them all. He knows exactly the cost of choosing such a path. Although His advice to us may seem unduly harsh, His thoughts on the matter have never changed: *"If any man will come after me, let him deny himself, and take up his cross daily, and follow me."* (Luk. 9:23).

The wide and broad gate leading to death and destruction may indeed be easier and more pleasurable, but there is little joy or profit derived from it. Solomon, the wisest man in his time, describes this type of mentality as meaningless and unproductive:

"When I surveyed all that my hands had done and what I had toiled to achieve, everything was meaningless, a chasing after the wind; nothing was gained under the sun. So, I hated life, because the work that is done under the sun

was grievous to me. All of it is meaningless, a chasing after the wind. I hated all the things I had toiled for under the sun, because I must leave them to the one who comes after me." (Eccl. 2:11, 17-18).

The age-old dilemma of knowing what to believe, who to follow, and which path to take boils down to a matter of choice. The Lord gives us the free-will and wisdom to choose wisely which path to follow. For us, it is not a matter of choosing between a blue pill or red one, but rather choosing between life or death, blessings or curses, and good or evil.[61] James, the half-brother of Jesus, explained it this way: *"Show me your faith apart from your works, and I will show you my faith by my works."* (Jam. 2:18, ESV).

Knowing the path might be compared to having faith without any evidence of works to support it. Whereas, *walking the path* might be compared to having faith with evidence of works. James argued that faith—like the will of God and love of God—was both actionable and altruistic. It became *actionable* when it was coupled with the will of God. It became *altruistic* when it was motivated by the love of God, and our "unselfish concern for the welfare and well-being of others." (Merriam-Webster.com (c), 2020). Faith, coupled with the will and love of God, results in purpose or what some might call "an expected end." (Jer. 29:11).

The Bible is quite adamant that the Lord does not withhold secrets from those called by His name: *"Unto you it is given to know the mystery of the kingdom of God: but unto them that are without, all these things are done in parables: That seeing they may see, and not perceive; and hearing they may hear, and not understand; lest at any time they should be converted, and their sins should be forgiven them."* (Mrk. 4:11-12; Cp. Eph. 1:9-10).

Maintaining an intimate and amicable relationship with God, through Jesus Christ, is key to us having access to the wisdom and knowledge of God. The fact that many Christians profess to have relationship with Christ, and yet know so little about Him, was the basis of Jesus' harsh criticism of those default in their relationship with Him:

"Many will say to me in that day, Lord, Lord, have we not prophesied in thy name? And in thy name have cast out devils? And in thy name done many wonderful works? And then will I profess unto them, I never knew you: depart from me, ye that work iniquity." (Mat. 7:22-23).

Cause-and-Effect

We are living in a day and time where we can no longer trust what we see, feel, or hear. In many ways, the believer is the only living testament of Jesus Christ that many people will encounter in their lifetime. If we fail to exemplify who Jesus is, what He stood for, and all that He represented, then we not only fall short of the Lord's expectation of us, but also fail in our efforts to build and expand the Kingdom exponentially. It is important for us as believers to understand the Godly influence we possess as ambassadors for the Kingdom.

It has been said, when two or more events occur in a way that one event is the result of another—or one event cannot exist without a preceding event—they are said to have a cause-and-effect relationship to one another. (Reference, 2020). Paul is a prime example of cause-and-effect. In his former state as Saul of Tarsus, Paul's tyrannical behavior and unnecessary persecution of the early Christian church and disciples caused a disturbance in the Kingdom of God that effected the lives of thousands. Despite his irrational and turbulent behavior, the seed of God lying dormant inside him prompted a miraculous encounter with Jesus Christ while on the road to Damascus.

This one encounter so dramatically changed Paul's life that he not only changed his name from Saul to Paul, but he also became a powerful instrument in sharing the gospel with the Gentile nations. His in-depth and revelatory understanding of the body of Christ and the Kingdom of God inspired most of the writings of the New Testament.

It is through the life of Paul that we are privileged to know and abide under the Law of Grace.

The uniqueness of the *Law of Grace* is it spells out, in no uncertain terms, that God's mercy, grace, and favor is not selective but inclusive of *"whosoever will...take the water of life freely."* (Rev. 22:17b). Neither is it central to one group of people (the Jewish people) or one nation (the nation of Israel). Rather, *"everyone who believes that Jesus is the Christ has been born of God, and everyone who loves the Father, loves whoever has been born of him."* (1 Joh. 5:1, ESV; Cp. 1 Joh. 4:15, ESV).

Based on this, we can make the conjecture that anyone who loves God and is born of Him is no longer bound to or constrained by the Law of Moses.[62] Today, we abide under a new and more glorious covenant (the Law of Grace) dictated by the finished work of Jesus Christ. The fact that God's mercy, favor, and grace is available to any and all who believe in Him gives us peace. A *"peace of God which transcends all understanding."* (Phil. 4:7, NIV).

Spiritual Legacy and Engagement

Legacy is not solely a matter of what we inherit. It is also a matter of what we pass on to those who come behind us, as a consequence of what we have inherited. It is a form of transference, a rite of passage, and a changing of the guard, where the old (former things) makes way for the new (latter things). For those who are older, it is an opportunity to provide guidance and wisdom to the young, to equip them for their future. For those who are younger, it is an opportunity to seek guidance and glean wisdom from those who are older and more experienced at life.

From the believer's standpoint, the ramifications of legacy are far greater than what we can imagine. As *"heirs of God and joint-heirs with Christ"* (Rom. 8:17), we are connected to the legacy of Jesus Christ and all that He represents. Therefore, we are not called to be ordinary or live ordinary lives. We have a personal stake in the entitlements and responsibilities associated with Christ. So then, simply by reason of our spiritual heritage, and who we are connected with, we are called to live an exemplary lifestyle and to be extraordinary people of influence and leadership.

What qualifies us to function in this manner is our ability to operate with the mind of God, to do what is right and righteous, and to set things in order on behalf of God and the Kingdom. In every possible way, we are to set the standard, embody the standard, and convey the standards that Jesus established and passed on, as a consequence of His legacy. Of course, none of this means anything if we do not know who we are, why we exist, or what our purpose is in relationship to Christ. When it comes to spiritual engagement specifically, we must be prepared and properly equipped to engage and invade the devil's territory, to find, rescue, and retrieve all who belong to God and are a part of Christ's flock.

Make no mistake about it, Jesus knows exactly who belongs to Him. We know this by reason of what He said while communing with the Father in prayer: *Of those whom You gave Me I have lost none."* (John 18:9, NKJV). Based on the caliber of Jesus' prayer, it is quite evident not everyone belongs to Christ. This begs to ask the question of whether everyone on earth will be saved. Contrary to what many believe and teach, the answer clearly is no. Of course, this has nothing to do with our Lord's intent, choice, or desire; for He is *"longsuffering [towards us] not willing that any should perish, but that all should come to repentance."* (2 Pet. 3:9). The reason not all will be saved is a matter of choice, that is, not all will accept Christ and His gift of salvation when it is extended to them.

Jesus said, *"My sheep hear my voice, and I know them, and they follow me: And I give unto them eternal life; and they shall never perish, neither shall any man pluck them out of my hand. My Father, which gave them me, is greater than all; and no man is able to pluck them out of my Father's hand. I and my Father are one."* (Joh. 10:27-30).

The above passage is confirmation that anyone who belongs to Christ will eventually hear His voice and follow Him, even if not right away. This alone should relieve us of the obligation to force the gospel on other people, as opposed to simply presenting them with the "good news" of the gospel, and allowing them to choose for themselves.

Spirit of Fruitfulness

Jesus said something striking that was foretelling of the type of people we are meant to be. He said, *"Wherefore by their fruits ye shall know them. Not everyone that saith unto me, Lord, Lord, shall enter into the kingdom of heaven; but he that doeth the will of my Father which is in heaven."* (Mat. 7:20-21). Jesus appears to suggest here that one of the major ways to identify those who are a part of His body is their fruitfulness.

What does it mean to be fruitful? Well, according to *CompellingTruth.org.*: "In Scripture, fruit is a metaphor used to describe the outward demonstration of one's inward disposition. Our fruit includes things like our behavior, attitude, words, and thoughts. Fruit can be either good or bad. Good fruit cannot be judged on mere external acts, [for the simple reason] it works from the inside out [and is evident through] a change in our disposition, attitudes, affections, and actions. It is a work of God's grace, [wherein] our essential being and character [are] changed, renewed, and progressively conformed to the image and likeness of Christ. (CompellingTruth.org, 2011-2020).

When Jesus returns, He is not coming back for any and everybody. He is coming back for His chosen elect, a remnant of people who are called by His name, bear His markings, and possess the power, skill, and means to rule over the Kingdom well: *"But the saints of the most High shall take the kingdom, and possess the kingdom for ever, even for ever and ever."* (Dan. 7:18).

The Bible also foreshadows this expectation through the example of Moses: *"And Moses chose able men out of all Israel, and made them heads over the people, rulers of thousands, rulers of hundreds, rulers of fifties, and rulers of tens."* (Exo. 18:2).

What Moses achieved in the natural, Jesus will one day accomplish on all realms, naturally, spiritually, and universally: *"And I saw a new heaven and a new earth: for the first heaven and the first earth were passed away; and there was no more sea. And I John saw the holy city, new Jerusalem, coming down from God out of heaven, prepared as a bride adorned for her husband. And I heard a great voice out of heaven saying, Behold, the tabernacle of God is with men, and he will dwell with them, and they shall be his people, and God himself shall be with them, and be their God. And God shall wipe away all tears from their eyes; and there shall be no more death, neither sorrow, nor crying, neither shall there be any more pain: for the former things are passed away. And he that sat upon the throne said, Behold, I make all things new..."* (Rev. 21:1-5a).

Do you know who you are in Christ or who Christ is in you? Which path in life are you following? Is it the one leading to life and blessings, or death and destruction? The Bible says, *"No one born of God makes a practice of sinning, for God's seed abides in him, and he cannot keep on sinning because he has been born of God. By this it is evident who are the children of God, and who are the children of the devil: whoever does not practice righteousness is not of God, nor is the one who does not love his brother."* (1 Joh. 3:9-10, ESV).

Final Thoughts

You are not here by accident and you are not a mistake. Everything about your life has been masterfully designed for a purpose. If you have a purpose, then you have value.

The only Person who can quantify and qualify your real value and purpose is Jesus Christ. Jesus said, "As I live... every knee shall bow to me, and every tongue shall confess to God." (Rom. 14:11). At some point, each of us must decide whether Christ is the answer or not.

If you are a *non-believer* and desire to receive Jesus Christ as your personal Lord and Savior, then pray this simple prayer with me: *"Lord Jesus, I come to you just as I am. I repent of every sin and transgression in my life and I ask Your forgiveness. Today, I openly confess and acknowledge You, Jesus, as my Lord and Savior. Sanctify my mind, body, soul and spirit. Transform me into a perfect image and reflection of You. Help me to live for Your glory from this day forward. Thank you, Lord, for hearing my prayer and making me a part of your family. I ask these things in Jesus name, I pray. Amen."* If you prayed that prayer in sincerity, then you are saved! Welcome to the family of God!

If you are a *believer* and currently do not know your purpose or calling in Christ, then I encourage you to spend time in His presence, for only the Lord can reveal the nature of such things to you. I would strongly encourage you to do so because God has assigned a certain number of people to you, who are called to speak and sow into their lives. For every day you neglect to do so, someone is missing out on the blessings and gifts that only you can offer. I implore you, diligently seek after the Lord with all your mind, soul and spirit, for He alone holds the keys to unlock the mysteries of your life.

In closing, I want to thank all the readers who faithfully accompanied me on this journey. I hope you will entertain the possibility of reading my next book, *Living For A Purpose: The Seed Inside My Story,* with an anticipated publication date of Fall-Winter 2021. In the second book, I delve into the challenges of depression, what the root cause of mine was, how it deeply impacted my life, how the Lord delivered me from it, and how the Lord worked through the gift of writing to reveal the greatness of His seed lying dormant inside my story.

As I reflect over the last seventeen or more years, I feel sense of accomplishment, knowing that it was the Lord who granted me the grace and endurance to run this race and finish it. I hope in some small way, this book will spark conversations about your life journey; and that those conversations will be as meaningful to you, as my conversations with the Lord was to me. Until we meet again, stay focused, stay well, and may the grace and peace of God be your portion!

Acknowledgments

Words cannot express how deeply grateful I am for the wisdom, guidance, and revelation of the Holy Spirit who diligently guided my thoughts and words throughout this entire writing process.

I thank God for my parents, the late Mr. and Mrs. Ralph L. Walker, who played a crucial role in creating the person I am today. Heartfelt thanks and much love to all the family members and friends who supported my vision, continuously prayed for me, and encouraged me every step of the way. I love you and am indebted to you.

Special thanks to my advisers, Rev. Dr. Keith A. Savage, Dr. Cheryl A. Hill, and Pastor Georgette Prime-Godwin, who served as my anchors during this process, in holding me accountable to the Word of God.

Last but not least, special thanks to T. Carol Patterson for her editorial support and excellence, as well as Germaine Miller-Summers of *Hope of Vision Publishing* for her publishing advice, support, and encouragement.

About the Author

Writing under the pseudonym of *B. Toliver Walker* to honor her parents, Bettye draws from a myriad of life experiences and deeply profound spiritual encounters to encourage generations of believers and non-believers alike. Her gift for writing introspectively, in partnership with the Holy Spirit, was birthed out of her obedience to the Lord to write on the topic of *Living For A Purpose*.

Her passion for motivating, building, and developing people began with a voluntary role as a Conflicts Negotiator, Mediator, and Advocate of employee/employer conflicts at a Virginia-based law firm. It was during her six-year term as a volunteer that she began to study and observe the systemic effects of broken infrastructures, broken relationships, broken forms of communications, and all the people who became broken as a result of it. This inspired her pursuit of a Masters' in *Human Services Counseling,* at the age of 59, which she completed in one year.

After leaving the workforce in 2013, she established *B.WalkerConsultants*, a human services consulting company, specializing in personal development, conflict negotiations, and motivational-editorial coaching. The company's vision is, *"to build and connect human capacity and capabilities on a global scale,"* through self-awareness, introspection, and behavior management. In 1990's, she founded a 501(c)(3) non-profit organization called the *Brothers and Sisters In Christ Project* ("The BASIC Project"). The vision of behind her non-profit is, *"to transform lives, communities, and organizations through Kingdom leadership."*

Professionally, Bettye has more than four decades of combined experience in legal, corporate governance, non-profit management, process improvement, office administration, book publishing, and design. She holds a Bachelor's in Graphic Design from *Norfolk State University,* a Masters' in Human Services Counseling from *Regent University,* attended *Pratt Institute* for three years, studying Communications Design, and was licensed and ordained for the work of ministry in 1966, by the *Deliverance Evangelistic Centers, Inc.* in Newark, N.J. Today, she continues to inspire and motivate others through her example, behavior, and words of encouragement.

References

Basden, Andrew. (2009, Jan 1). Radah. Retrieved from http://kgsvr.net/xn/radah.html.

Blue Letter Bible Online. (2020). Epithymia (G1939). Strong's Greek Lexicon (KJV). Retrieved from https://www.blueletterbible.org//lang/lexicon/lexicon.cfm?Strongs=G1939&t=KJV.

Catholic Answers. (1996-2020). Q&A: Why did God change Saul's name to Paul? Retrieved from https://www.catholic.com/qa/why-did-god-change-sauls-name-to-paul.

CompellingTruth.org. (2011-2020). What is meant by being a fruitful Christian? Retrieved from https://www.compellingtruth.org/fruitful-Christian.html.

Focus 3, LLC. (2019). What does discipline mean? Blog: Focus 3. Retrieved from https://www.focus3.com/blog/what-does-discipline-mean.

Genius Media Group, Inc. (2020). Dionne Warwick: A house is not a home lyrics. Retrieved from https://genius.com/Dionne-warwick-a-house-is-not-a-home-lyrics.

Law, Jeannie. (2019, Jul. 24). God don't mean people to own people: Upcoming Harriet Tubman biopic highlights faith of abolitionist. The Christian Post. Retrieved from https://www.christianpost.com/news/god-dont-mean-people-to-own-people-upcoming-harriet-tubman-biopic-highlights-faith-of-abolitionist.html.

Long, Phillip J. (2013, Feb. 10). Why did Saul persecute the Jewish Christians. Blog: Reading Acts. Retrieved from https://readingacts.com/2013/02/10/why-did-saul-persecute-the-jewish-christians.

McClure, P. Rosenwald Schools. (2018, Apr. 3). Rosenwald Schools. In Encyclopedia Virginia. Retrieved from http://www.EncyclopediaVirginia.org/Rosenwald_Schools.

Merriam-Wester.com (a) (2019) Providence. In the Merriam-Webster.com Dictionary. Retrieved December 12, 2019 from https://www.merriamwebster.com/dictionary / providence.

Merriam-Wester.com (b) (2019) Mandate. In the Merriam-Webster.com Dictionary. Retrieved December 12, 2019 from https://www.merriam-webster.com/dictionary/mandate.

Merriam-Wester.com (c) (2020) Altruistic. In the Merriam-Webster.com Dictionary. Retrieved March 5, 2020 from https://www.merriam-webster.com/dictionary/altruistic.

Nee, Watchman (a). (1968, 1977). The Spiritual Man – Vol 1; Part One: Introduction on Spirit, Soul and Body; Chap 1: Spirit, Soul and Body. Pgs. 26-27. Christian Fellowship Publishers, Inc.: New York.

Nee, Watchman (b). (1968, 1977). The Spiritual Man – Vol 1; Part Four: The Spirit; Chap 1: The Holy Spirit and the Believer's Spirit. Pgs. 14-15. Christian Fellowship Publishers, Inc.: New York.

NetBibleStudy.com. (n.d.). A Study of the Tabernacle – Lesson I. Retrieved from http://www.netbiblestudy.com/00_cartimages/Tab-lesson-1.pdf.

Oxford English Dictionary Online (OED) (a). (2019, Dec.) Usurp (v.2a). Oxford University Press. Accessed January 23, 2020 from https://www.oed.com/view/Entry/220720?rskey=m3yQfv&result=2&isAdvanced=false.

Oxford English Dictionary Online (OED) (b). (2019, Dec.) Defy (v.4) Oxford University Press. Accessed January 23, 2020 from https://www.oed.com/view/Entry/49035?rskey=7ZCoED &result=2.

Psychology Today. (2020). Adolescence. Sussex Publishers, LLC. Retrieved from https://www.psychologytoday.com/us/basics/adolescence.

Reference (2020). What does cause and effect mean? Ask Media Group, LLC. Retrieved from https://www.reference.com/science/cause-effect-mean-269a3a0f9685f064.

Tverberg, Lois. (2016, Aug. 25). What Is Jesus Real Name? Blogsite: Our Rabbi Jesus. Retrieved from https://declarehissplendour.wordpress.com/2016/08/25/what-is-jesus-real-name.

Tsdempster1. (2013, Apr. 7). Matrix 09: Knowing the Path & Walking the Path. YouTube. Retrieved from https://youtu.be/fHjMhYoY4Mg.

Strong's Greek Lexicon (a). (2020). G37: Hagiazō. (KJV). Retrieved January 20, 2020 from https://www.blueletterbible.org//lang/lexicon/lexicon.cfm?Strongs=G37&t=KJV.

Strong's Greek Lexicon (b). (2020). G5046: Teleios (KJV). Retrieved January 20, 2020 from https://www.blueletterbible.org//lang/lexicon/lexicon.cfm?Strongs=G5046&t=KJV.

Strong's Greek Lexicon (c). (2020). G3648: Holoklēros. (KJV). Retrieved January 20, 2020 from https://www.blueletterbible.org//lang/lexicon/lexicon.cfm?Strongs=G3648&t=KJV.

Wikipedia. (2020, Feb. 1). Code of conduct. Retrieved from https://en.wikipedia.org/wiki/ Code_of_conduct.

Endnotes

1 Romans 8:35-39
2 John 4:13-15; John 6:35; Revelations 21:6
3 Romans 8:28
4 Isaiah 30:15
5 Philippians 2:5; Romans 12:2
6 Psalm 119:133
7 1 Corinthians 9:27
8 Roman 12:2
9 1 Corinthians 15:58
10 Matthew 5:13
11 1 Timothy 2:5.
12 Ephesians 4:11
13 1 Corinthians 12:28
14 Matthew 9:35; Matthew 24:14
15 Romans 12:4; 1 Corinthians 12:5, 12, 20
16 1 Peter 2:9
17 2 Corinthians 4:7; 2 Timothy 2:20
18 Mark 6:10; Luke 11:2
19 Exodus 19:6; 1 Peter 2:9; Hebrews 8:1-2
20 Romans 4:4-5
21 1 Peter 2:9; Matthew 16:16-18
22 Mark 9:50
23 1 Peter 2:2
24 2 Tim. 2:15; Rev. 22:14
25 Mark 4:20
26 Act 1:8
27 Acts 17:28a
28 Genesis 1:26-31; 2:1-25.
29 1 John 3:2
30 1 Corinthians 12:31
31 1 Tim. 2:5; Cp. 1 Cor. 8:6; Joh. 17:11
32 John 13:12-15
33 Genesis 1:26; Matthew 12:43-45; 1 Peter 5:8-9
34 https://www.watchmannee.org

35 John 3:3, 7-8
36 John 14:26
37 2 Timothy 2:21
38 John 3:3, 7; 1 Peter 1:23; Hebrews 5:13
39 1 Corinthians 3:1; Hebrews 5:13
40 1 Peter 2:2; Jeremiah 1:5
41 2 Peter 3:16
42 1 Peter 2:25
43 Romans 8:7; 1 Corinthians 3:3
44 Revelations 3:15-16
45 Galatians 5:24; Romans 1:21-32
46 John 4:34; Hebrews 5:12
47 Hebrews 5:12-13
48 John 6:33, 48
49 Romans 12:2
50 Revelations 3:20
51 Exodus 19:5
52 Matthew 16:24
53 Titus 2:7; John 14:12
54 Ephesians 4:13
55 Matthew 24:24
56 https://www.goodreads.com/quotes/7109-that-s-one-small-step-for-a-man-one-giant-leap
57 John 1:1-4, 14
58 Romans 8:33; Luke 18:7
59 Proverbs 2:10-22
60 Hebrews 4:15
61 Deuteronomy 30:14-15, 19
62 2 Corinthians 3:7-18

Photo Credits

Figure 1: Old Testament Tabernacle; Accessed April 24, 2020 from Yahoo public domain. Retrieved from https://images.search.yahoo.com/yhs/search?p=photos+of+the+old+testament+tabernacle.

www.ingramcontent.com/pod-product-compliance
Lightning Source LLC
Chambersburg PA
CBHW070504170726
48291CB00008B/2643

* 9 7 8 1 9 4 2 8 7 1 7 5 0 *